1986

S0-BRA-897

Collected poems/

3  0301  00089364  0

# COLLECTED POEMS

# Collected Poems

CHARLES TOMLINSON

LIBRARY
College of St. Francis
JOLIET, ILLINOIS

Oxford   New York
OXFORD UNIVERSITY PRESS
1985

Oxford University Press, Walton Street, Oxford OX2 6DP

Oxford  New York  Toronto
Delhi  Bombay  Calcutta  Madras  Karachi
Kuala Lumpur  Singapore  Hong Kong  Tokyo
Nairobi  Dar es Salaam  Cape Town
Melbourne  Auckland

and associated companies in
Beirut  Berlin  Ibadan  Nicosia

Oxford is a trade mark of Oxford University Press

© Charles Tomlinson 1985

All rights reserved. No part of this publication may be reproduced,
stored in a retrieval system, or transmitted, in any form or by any means,
electronic, mechanical, photocopying, recording, or otherwise, without
the prior permission of Oxford University Press

British Library Cataloguing in Publication Data
Tomlinson, Charles
Charles Tomlimson: Collected Poems
I. Title
821'.914   PR6039.03479
ISBN 0-19-211974-5

Library of Congress Cataloging in Publication Data
Tomlinson, Charles, 1927–
Collected poems, 1951–1981
I. Title
PR6039.0349A6 1985   821'.914   85–3016
ISBN 0-19-211974-5

Set by Latimer Trend & Company Ltd.
Printed in Great Britain by
St. Edmundsbury Press Ltd.
Bury St. Edmunds, Suffolk

821.914
T657

80.068

121,021

*For Brenda, Justine and Juliet*

# *Preface*

In 1951 I published with the Hand and Flower Press my first pamphlet of verse, *Relations and Contraries*. Except for the title and 'Poem' ('Wakening with the window over fields') there is little I wish to rescue from that collection. 'Poem' stands in the present volume as a kind of prelude to what follows. I realized, when I wrote it, that I was approaching the sort of thing I wanted to do, where space represented possibility and where self would have to embrace that possibility somewhat self-forgetfully, putting aside the more possessive and violent claims of personality. The embrace was, all the same, a passionate one, or so it seemed to me. The title *Relations and Contraries* proved to contain a dialectic very fundamental for subsequent poems.

I reprint here my collections in the order of their appearance. The text of *Seeing is Believing* is the British text of 1960. The book first appeared in New York in 1958. The later edition excludes one poem and adds several others. I have removed misprints throughout these *Collected Poems* and there are revisions in *Written on Water*—three lines of 'Veneris Venefica Agrestis', one of 'October'. My greatest debt is to my wife, for whom all these books were written in the first place.

# Contents

xiii

*The Way In and Other Poems* (1974)

*The Shaft* (1978)

*The Flood* (1981)

## *Poem*

Wakening with the window over fields
To the coin-clear harness-jingle as a float
Clips by, and each succeeding hoof fall, now remote,
Breaks clean and frost-sharp on the unstopped ear.

The hooves describe an arabesque on space,
A dotted line in sound that falls and rises
As the cart goes by, recedes, turns to retrace
Its way back through the unawakened village.

And space vibrates, enlarges with the sound;
Though space is soundless, yet creates
From very soundlessness a ground
To counterstress the lilting hoof fall as it breaks.

# THE NECKLACE
## (1955)

*The necklace is a carving not a kiss*
WALLACE STEVENS

## Aesthetic

Reality is to be sought, not in concrete,
But in space made articulate:
The shore, for instance,
Spreading between wall and wall;
The sea-voice
Tearing the silence from the silence.


## Venice

Cut into by doors
The morning assumes night's burden,
The houses assemble in tight cubes.

From the palace flanking the waterfront
She is about to embark, but pauses.
Her dress is a veil of sound
Extended upon silence.

Under the bridge,
Contained by the reflected arc
A tunnel of light
Effaces walls, water, horizon.

Floating upon its own image
A cortège of boats idles through space.


# Nine Variations in a Chinese Winter Setting

### I
Warm flute on the cold snow
Lays amber in sound.

### II
Against brushed cymbal
Grounds yellow on green,
Amber on tinkling ice.

3

## III

The sage beneath the waterfall
Numbers the blessing of a flute;
Water lets down
Exploding silk.

## IV

The hiss of raffia,
The thin string scraped with the back of the bow
Are not more bat-like
Than the gusty bamboos
Against a flute.

## V

Pine-scent
In snow-clearness
Is not more exactly counterpointed
Than the creak of trodden snow
Against a flute.

## VI

The outline of the water-dragon
Is not embroidered with so intricate a thread
As that with which the flute
Defines the tangible borders of a mood.

## VII

The flute in summer makes streams of ice:
In winter it grows hospitable.

## VIII

In mist, a flute is cold
Beside a flute in snow.

## IX

Degrees of comparison
Go with differing conditions:
Sunlight mellows lichens,
Whereas snow mellows the flute.

# Eight Observations on the Nature of Eternity

### I

You would not think the room
(Grown small as a honey pot
And filled with a slow yellow light)
Could so burden itself with the afternoon.

### II

It is neither between three and four
Nor is it time for the lamps:
It is afternoon—interminably.

### III

Elsewhere there is sky, movement or a view,
Here there is light, stillness and no dimension.

### IV

The afternoon violet
Is not so unthinkably itself,
Nor does that imperceptibly greening light
Freeze so remotely in its own essence
As this yellow.

### V

Red flowers
Detonate and go out
At the curtain fringe.

### VI

Objects regard us for the last time,
The window, that enemy of solitude,
Looks inward.

### VII

Jaws of unhurried shade
Yawn on the masonry.

### VIII

We will light no candles:
What is to be will be.
The room is merging
Into a moonless landscape.

# Suggestions for the Improvement of a Sunset

Darkening the edges of the land,
Imperceptibly it must drain out colours
Drawing all light into its centre.

Six points of vantage provide us with six sunsets.

The sea partakes of the sky. It is less
Itself than the least pool which, if threatened,
Prizes lucidity.

The pond is lime-green, an enemy
Of gold, bearing no change but shadow.

Seen from above, the house would resemble
A violin, abandoned, and lost in its own darkness;

Diminished, through the wrong end of a glass,
A dice ambushed by lowering greens;

Accorded its true proportions,
The stone would give back the light
Which, all day, it has absorbed.

The after-glow, broken by leaves and windows,
Confirms green's triumph against yellow.


# Sea Change

To define the sea—
We change our opinions
With the changing light.

Light struggles with colour:
A quincunx
Of five stones, a white
Opal threatened by emeralds.

The sea is uneasy marble.

The sea is green silk.

The sea is blue mud, churned
By the insistence of wind.

Beneath dawn a sardonyx may be cut from it
In white layers laced with a carnelian orange,
A leek- or apple-green chalcedony
Hewn in the cold light.

Illustration is white wine
Floating in a saucer of ground glass
On a pedestal of cut glass:

A static instance, therefore untrue.

## Through Binoculars

In their congealed light
We discover that what we had taken for a face
Has neither eyes nor mouth,
But only the impersonality of anatomy.

Silencing movement,
They withdraw life.

Definition grows clear-cut, but bodiless,
Withering by a dimension.

To see thus
Is to ignore the revenge of light on shadow,
To confound both in a brittle and false union.

This fictive extension into madness
Has a kind of bracing effect:
That normality is, after all, desirable
One can no longer doubt having experienced its opposite.

Binoculars are the last phase in a romanticism:
The starkly mad vision, not mortal,
But dangling one in a vicarious, momentary idiocy.

To dispense with them
Is to make audible the steady roar of evening,
Withdrawing in slow ripples of orange,
Like the retreat of water from sea-caves.

# Montage

The cheval-glass is empty
The sky is a blank screen.

In the buried room
They look back upon themselves.

The comity of three objects
Builds stillness within stillness.

The scene terminates without words
A tower collapsing upon feathers.

# Dialogue

She:    It turns on its axis.

He:    To say that it was round
Would be to ignore what is within.
The transparent framework of cells,
The constellation of flashes.

She:    It reveals the horizon.

He:    It surrounds it,
Transmits and refines it
Through a frozen element:
A taut line crossing a pure white.

She:    It contains distance.

He:    It distances what is near,
Transforms the conversation piece
Into a still life,
Isolates, like the end of a corridor.

She:    It is the world of contour:

He:    The black outline separating brilliances
That would otherwise fuse,
A single flame.

She:   If it held personages—

He:    They would be minute,
       Their explicit movements
       The mosaic which dances.

Both:  In unison, they would clarify
       The interior of the fruit,
       The heart of the cut stone.


# *Flute Music*

There is a moment for speech and for silence.
Lost between possibilities
But deploring a forced harmony,
We elect the flute.

A season, defying gloss, may be the sum
Of blue water beneath green rain;
It may comprise comets, days, lakes
Yet still bear the exegesis of music.

Seeing and speaking we are two men:
The eye encloses as a window—a flute
Governs the land, its winter and its silence.

The flute is uncircumscribed by moonlight or irised
                                    mornings.
It moves with equal certainty
Through a register of palm-greens and flesh-rose.

The glare of brass over a restless bass
(Red glow across olive twilight)
Urges to a delighted excess,
A weeping among broken gods.

The flute speaks (reason's song
Riding the ungovernable wave)
The bound of passion
Out of the equitable core of peace.

# The Bead

At the clear core, morning
Extinguishes everything save light.

Breaking the spectrum
Threads cross, flare, emerge
Like the glitter of dust before stained windows.

Turned in the shadow
It is a black diamond
Containing nothing but itself.

The idea dissolves in passion:
The light holds,
Circling the cold centre.

# The Death of the Infanta

### for Donald Davie

Outside, upon warm air,
The impingement of strollers and public flowers.

Between the cold walls
You would say that space, also, was stone.

The perspective hollows itself into the distance
Littered with chairs and statues.

Her room you would suppose
The ultimate box held by the others,
Her person, the final space.

But you would err. Her glass
Catches the finale of both.

# The Art of Poetry

At first, the mind feels bruised.
The light makes white holes through the black foliage
Or mist hides everything that is not itself.

But how shall one say so?—
The fact being, that when the truth is not good enough
We exaggerate. Proportions

Matter. It is difficult to get them right.
There must be nothing
Superfluous, nothing which is not elegant
And nothing which is if it is merely that.

This green twilight has violet borders.

Yellow butterflies
Nervously transferring themselves
From scarlet to bronze flowers
Disappear as the evening appears.


## Observation of Facts

Facts have no eyes. One must
Surprise them, as one surprises a tree
By regarding its (shall I say?)
Facets of copiousness.

The tree stands.

The house encloses.

The room flowers.

These are fact stripped of imagination:
Their relation is mutual.

A dryad is a sort of chintz curtain
Between myself and a tree.
The tree stands: or does not stand:
As I draw, or remove the curtain.

The house encloses: or fails to signify
As being bodied over against one,
As something one has to do with.

11

The room flowers once one has introduced
Mental fibre beneath its elegance,
A rough pot or two, outweighing
The persistence of frippery
In lampshades or wallpaper.

Style speaks what was seen,
Or it conceals the observation
Behind the observer: a voice
Wearing a ruff.

Those facets of copiousness which I proposed
Exist, do so when we have silenced ourselves.


## *Fiascherino*

Over an ash-fawn beach fronting a sea which keeps
    Rolling and unrolling, lifting
The green fringes from submerged rocks
    On its way in, and, on its way out
Dropping them again, the light

Squanders itself, a saffron morning
    Advances among foam and stones, sticks
Clotted with black naphtha
    And frayed to the newly carved
Fresh white of chicken flesh.

One leans from the cliff-top. Height
    Distances like an inverted glass; the shore
Is diminished but concentrated, jewelled
    With the clarity of warm colours
That, seen more nearly, would dissipate

Into masses. The map-like interplay
    Of sea-light against shadow
And the mottled close-up of wet rocks
    Drying themselves in the hot air
Are lost to us. Content with our portion,

Where, we ask ourselves, is the end of all this
   Variety that follows us? Glare
Pierces muslin; its broken rays
   Hovering in trembling filaments
Glance on the ceiling with no more substance

Than a bee's wing. Thickening, these
   Hang down over the pink walls
In green bars, and, flickering between them,
   A moving fan of two colours,
The sea unrolls and rolls itself into the low room.

# SEEING IS BELIEVING
## (1958, 1960)

*To*
*Donald and Hugh*
*who saw and believed*

# The Atlantic

Launched into an opposing wind, hangs
   Grappled beneath the onrush,
And there, lifts, curling in spume,
   Unlocks, drops from that hold
Over and shoreward. The beach receives it,
   A whitening line, collapsing
Powdering-off down its broken length;
   Then, curded, shallow, heavy
With clustering bubbles, it nears
   In a slow sheet that must climb
Relinquishing its power, upward
   Across tilted sand. Unravelled now
And the shore, under its lucid pane,
   Clear to the sight, it is spent:
The sun rocks there, as the netted ripple
   Into whose skeins the motion threads it
Glances athwart a bed, honey-combed
   By heaving stones. Neither survives the instant
But is caught back, and leaves, like the after-image
   Released from the floor of a now different mind,
A quick gold, dyeing the uncovering beach
   With sunglaze. That which we were,
Confronted by all that we are not,
   Grasps in subservience its replenishment.

# Winter Encounters

House and hollow; village and valley-side:
   The ceaseless pairings, the interchange
In which the properties are constant
   Resumes its winter starkness. The hedges' barbs
Are bared. Lengthened shadows
   Intersecting, the fields seem parcelled smaller
As if by hedgerow within hedgerow. Meshed
   Into neighbourhood by such shifting ties,
The house reposes, squarely upon its acre
   Yet with softened angles, the responsive stone
Changeful beneath the changing light:
   There is a riding-forth, a voyage impending

In this ruffled air, where all moves
   Towards encounter. Inanimate or human,
The distinction fails in these brisk exchanges—
   Say, merely, that the roof greets the cloud,
Or by the wall, sheltering its knot of talkers,
   Encounter enacts itself in the conversation
On customary subjects, where the mind
   May lean at ease, weighing the prospect
Of another's presence. Rain
   And the probability of rain, tares
And their progress through a field of wheat—
   These, though of moment in themselves,
Serve rather to articulate the sense
   That having met, one meets with more
Than the words can witness. One feels behind
   Into the intensity that bodies through them
Calmness within the wind, the warmth in cold.


# *Reflections*

Like liquid shadows. The ice is thin
   Whose mirror smears them as it intercepts
Withdrawing colours; and where the crust,
   As if a skin livid with tautening scars,
Whitens, cracks, it steals from these deformations
   A style too tenuous for the image. A mirror lies, and
Flawed like this, may even lie with art,
   With reticence: 'I exaggerate nothing,
For the reflections—scarcely half you see—
   Tell nothing of what you feel.' Nature is blind
Like habit. Distrust them. We, since no mirrors,
   Are free both to question this deployment
And to arrange it—what we reflect
   Being what we choose. Though without deference,
We are grateful. When we perceive, as keen
   As the bridge itself, a bridge inlaying the darkness
Of smooth water, our delight acknowledges our debt—
   To nature, from whom we choose;
And, fencing that fullness back, to habit,
   The unsheathed image piercing our winter sleep.

## Ponte Veneziano
### Two figures

Tight-socketed in space, they watch
Drawn by a single glance,
Stripping the vista to its depth.

A prow pinpoints them:
They stare beyond it. The canopy
Which shades a boat
Flares from the line through which they gaze
Orange against coolness.

They do not see it, or,
Seeing, relegate the glow
To that point which it must occupy.

Undistracted, their glance channels itself
Ignoring the whiteness of a bridge
To cross beneath, where,
Closed by the vault,
It broods on the further light.

They do not exclaim,
But, bound to that distance,
Transmit without gesture
Their stillness into its ringed centre.


## Oxen: Ploughing at Fiesole

The heads, impenetrable
And the slow bulk
Soundless and stooping,
A white darkness—burdened
Only by sun, and not
By the matchwood yoke—
They groove in ease
The meadow through which they pace
Tractable. It is as if
Fresh from the escape,
They consent to submission,
The debris of captivity
Still clinging there

Unnoticed behind those backs:
'But we submit'—the tenor
Unambiguous in that stride
Of even confidence—
'Giving and not conceding
Your premises. Work
Is necessary, therefore—'
(With an unsevered motion
Holding the pauses
Between stride and stride)
'We will be useful
But we will not be swift: now
Follow us for your improvement
And at our pace.' This calm
Bred from this strength, and the reality
Broaching no such discussion,
The man will follow, each
As the other's servant
Content to remain content.


# The Mediterranean

## I

In this country of grapes
Where the architecture
Plays musical interludes, flays
The emotions with the barest statement
Or, confusing the issue and the beholder,
Bewilders with an excessive formality,
There is also the sea.

## II

              The sea
Whether it is 'wrinkled' and 'crawls'
Or pounds, plunders, rounding
On itself in thunderous showers, a
Broken, bellowing foam canopy
Rock-riven and driven wild
By its own formless griefs—the sea
Carries, midway, its burning stripe of light.

### III

This country of grapes
Is a country, also, of trains, planes and gasworks.
'Tramway and palace' rankles. It is an idea
Neither the guidebook nor the imagination
Tolerates. The guidebook half lies
Of 'twenty minutes in a comfortable bus'
Of 'rows of cypresses, an
Uninterrupted series of matchless sights.'
The imagination cannot lie. It bites brick;
Says: 'This is steel—I will taste steel.

Bred on a lie, I am merely
Guidebooks, advertisements, politics.'

The sea laps by the railroad tracks.
To have admitted this also defines the sea.


## *Distinctions*

The seascape shifts.

Between the minutest interstices of time
Blue is blue.

A pine-branch
Tugs at the eye: the eye
Returns to grey-blue, blue-black or indigo
Or it returns, simply,
To blue-after-the-pine-branch.

Here, there is no question of aberrations
Into pinks, golds or mauves:
This is the variation Pater indicated
But failed to prove.

Art exists at a remove.
Evocation, at two,
Discusses a blue that someone
Heard someone talking about.

# Variant on a Scrap of Conversation

'There's nothing at all to be said for the day. ....'

Except that through the wet panes
Objects arrange themselves,
Blue tessellations, faintly irised
Dividing the room
Into an observed music.

As one approaches the windows
Fugues of colour
May be derived from a familiar interior,
A chair may be segmented and reassembled
In two steps.

To challenge the accepted vision
A further instance would be the wine-stopper,
Its head (cut into facets)
An eye for the cubist.

# Icos

White, a shingled path
Climbs among dusted olives
To where at the hill-crest
Stare houses, whiter
Than either dust or shingle.
The view, held from this vantage
Unsoftened by distance, because
Scoured by a full light,
Draws lucid across its depth
The willing eye: a beach,
A surf-line, broken
Where reefs meet it, into the heaving
Blanched rims of bay-arcs;
Above, piercing the empty blue,
A gull would convey whiteness
Through the sole space which lacks it
But, there, scanning the shore,
Hangs only the eagle, depth
Measured within its level gaze.

# How Still the Hawk

How still the hawk
Hangs innocent above
Its native wood:
Distance, that purifies the act
Of all intent, has graced
Intent with beauty.
Beauty must lie
As innocence must harm
Whose end (sited,
Held) is naked
Like the map it cowers on.
And the doom drops:
Plummet of peace
To him who does not share
The nearness and the need,
The shrivelled circle
Of magnetic fear.

# Object in a Setting

## I

From an empty sky
The morning deceives winter
With shadows and cold sapphire.

## II

Astral, clear:
To wish it a more human image
Is to mistake its purpose.

Silent:
It is the marble city without trees.

Translucent, focal:
It is the city one may hold on the palm
Or lift, veined, against the sun.

Faceted, irised, burning:
It is the glass stair
To the hanging gardens.

## III
The days turn to one their hard surfaces
Over which a glacial music
Pauses, renews, expands.


## *The Mausoleum*

It is already six. From the steeple
    The even tones of a steady chime
Greet with their punctuality our lateness.
    The hall is shut. But one may
Visit the mausoleum in its now public grove
    Without cost or hindrance, and
With half as many steps as one would lose
    Were one to proceed. Here is the turning.

The trees thin and one sees its pyramid
    A steep roof tapering above stone steps.
Climb them. It is empty. The dead
    Have buried their dead and the living
Can approach it without fear and push open
    (As one may find it) the frayed door
To stand where a child might and where children do
    Play under the bare shelves of stone tiers.

We enter, the sunlight just about
    To fade on the wall and, from its glowing ground,
A blurred shadow detaches itself hovering
    And cannot decide whether a green or blue
Will the more grace its momentary existence
    Or whether a shot-red could invade
Decorously so impoverished a kingdom.

The light withdraws and the shadow softens
    Until it floats unnameably, gathered up
Into the colourless medium of early dusk:
    It is then that the eye, putting aside
Such distractions can move earnestly
    Past the slung swag, chipped where it hangs
Under a white tablet, and slowly
    Climb upwards with its burden of questions.

For the tablet-square, remotely white
    But yellowed as if an effect of ivory
That has aged and which age has cracked,
    Proffers, scarified like the swag beneath it,
Unhealed wounds; ivory fractures
    But marble bruises, flakes, and these dark
Incursions, heavy with shade, are the work
    Of hands, recording such meanings as you shall read.

Were I a guide you would vouchsafe my legend
    Of how a race halted in tumult here
To exorcise in such a wavering light
    The authority of death, and by left-hand magic
Practised not against that but procreation,
    Signing each with his own name
Their composite work. But you must judge
    As you will and as the light permits.

For to grant to such fears their myth
    Is to distinguish them out of pity for a failing house.
Unleashed, it was no flickering colonnade
    Debouched this horde. The elegant swag
With the trim incision of the epitaphs no less
    Than the stone skull, mocked their impatience
And the blackened streets, the creeping architraves
    Of their Pandemonium, a city of mean years.

Swarming the base of the narrow walls
    As far as the raised arm can incise
Graffiti and beyond that as high as stone
    Can be aimed against stone in such a confine
The legend is complete however it is simple,
    Is plain, though under this dimmed
Clerestory the darkness liquefies it,
    And the work, however many the hands, one.

As surely as the air cooling and the scents
    That burn on the chillness at our exit,
The gravel rasping its trodden canon
    Under the weave of thought, usher us
Into that world to which this silence
    Scarred by so many hands is prologue,
You will concede that they have gained it whole
    Whatever they have lost in its possession.

121,021

25

LIBRARY
College of St. Francis
JOLIET, ILLINOIS

# Glass Grain

The glare goes down. The metal of a molten pane
Cast on the wall with red light burning through,
Holds in its firm, disordered square, the shifting strands
The glass conceals, till (splitting sun) it dances
Lanterns in lanes of light its own streaked image.
Like combed-down hair. Like weathered wood, where
Line, running with, crowds on line and swaying
Rounding each knot, yet still keeps keen
The perfect parallel. Like . . . in likes, what do we look for?
Distinctions? That, but not that in sum. Think of the fugue's theme:
After inversions and divisions, doors
That no keys can open, cornered conceits
Apprehensions, all ways of knowledge past,
Eden comes round again, the motive dips
Back to its shapely self, its naked nature
Clothed by comparison alone—related. We ask
No less, watching suggestions that a beam selects
From wood, from water, from a muslin-weave,
Swerving across our window, on our wall
(Transparency teased out) the grain of glass.

# Gli Scafari

Rock reproduces rock
In miniature
On rock; and where
The sheerness fails
Particularity resumes:
Layers, in flakes;
Piled shale; or
Minutest slates
Not slatted—packed and pitted
Against each
Barbarous element,
For all four
Climb with this sea
Save fire (and fire
Galls from above)

To will a corrosion
In so much silent decision among
Toy fortresses
Which can resist.

## *Tramontana at Lerici*

Today, should you let fall a glass it would
    Disintegrate, played off with such keenness
Against the cold's resonance (the sounds
    Hard, separate and distinct, dropping away
In a diminishing cadence) that you might swear
    This was the imitation of glass falling.

Leaf-dapples sharpen. Emboldened by this clarity
    The minds of artificers would turn prismatic,
Running on lace perforated in crisp wafers
    That could cut like steel. Constitutions,
Drafted under this fecund chill, would be annulled
    For the strictness of their equity, the moderation of their pity.

At evening, one is alarmed by such definition
    In as many lost greens as one will give glances to recover,
As many again which the landscape
    Absorbing into the steady dusk, condenses
From aquamarine to that slow indigo–pitch
    Where the light and twilight abandon themselves.

And the chill grows. In this air
    Unfit for politicians and romantics
Dark hardens from blue, effacing the windows:
    A tangible block, it will be no accessory
To that which does not concern it. One is ignored
    By so much cold suspended in so much night.

# Northern Spring

Nor is this the setting for extravagance. Trees
    Fight with the wind, the wind eludes them
Streaking its cross-lanes over the uneasy water
    Whose bronze whitens. To emulate such confusion
One must impoverish the resources of folly,
    But to taste it is medicinal. Consider

How through that broken calm, as the sun emerges,
    The sky flushes its blue, dyeing the grass
In the promise of a more stable tone:
    Less swift however than the cloud is wide—
Its shadow (already) quenching the verdure
    As its bulk muffles the sun—the blue drains
And the assault renews in colourless ripples.

Then, lit, the scene deepens. Where should one look
    In the profusion of possibilities? One conceives
Placing before them a square house
    Washed in the coolness of lime, a hub
For the scattered deployment, to define
    In pure white from its verdant ground
The variegated excess which threatens it.

Spring lours. Neither will the summer achieve
    That Roman season of an equable province
Where the sun is its own witness and the shadow
    Measures its ardour with the impartiality
Of the just. Evening, debauching this sky, asks
    To be appraised and to be withstood.


# The Gorge

Wind in the fleece of ivy
As, from above, the pilot
Sees water, moved by its currents.

But we are closer: he would miss
Such evident ripples
Like a conflagration
Climbing the rockface.

Light, swept perpendicular
Into the leaf-mass
Flickers out, only to reappear momentarily
Stippling remoter clumps.

The movement deceives, a surface
For silence, inaccessible
Inactivity. Even the sea
Shifts to its centre.

## On a Landscape by Li Ch'eng

Look down. There is snow.
Where the snow ends
Sea, and where the sea enters
Grey among capes
Like an unvaried sky, lapping
From finger to finger
Of a raised hand, travellers
Skirt between snow and sea.
Minute, furtive and exposed,
Their solitude is unchosen and will end
In comity, in talk
So seasoned by these extremes
It will recall stored fruits
Bitten by a winter fire.
The title, without disapprobation,
Says, 'Merchants.'

## The Crane

That insect, without antennae, over its
Cotton-spool lip, letting
An almost invisible tenuity
Of steel cable, drop
Some seventy feet, with the
Grappling hook hidden also
Behind a dense foreground
Among which it is fumbling, and
Over which, mantis-like

It is begging or threatening, gracile
From a clear sky—that paternal
Constructive insect, without antennae,
Would seem to assure us that
'The future is safe, because
It is in my hands.' And we do not
Doubt this veracity, we can only
Fear it—as many of us
As pause here to remark
Such silent solicitude
For lifting intangible weights
Into real walls.

## Paring the Apple

There are portraits and still-lifes.

And there is paring the apple.

And then? Paring it slowly,
From under cool-yellow
Cold-white emerging. And . . .?

The spring of concentric peel
Unwinding off white,
The blade hidden, dividing.

There are portraits and still-lifes
And the first, because 'human'
Does not excel the second, and
Neither is less weighted
With a human gesture, than paring the apple
With a human stillness.

The cool blade
Severs between coolness, apple-rind
Compelling a recognition.

# Rose-hips

Weather the frost, stir
At the cold's passing
Where white alone (were it not
For such drops of fire)
Would dominate, as the incessant
Massing of mist on mist
Draws-to over distance, leaving
Only a white of frost
On a white of fog, but
Deepened in dye by such
Candid obscurity, they stare
Sharper than summer berries
From this unlit air.


# More Foreign Cities

'Nobody wants any more poems about foreign cities...'
*(From a recent disquisition on poetics)*

Not forgetting Ko-jen, that
Musical city (it has
Few buildings and annexes
Space by combating silence),
There is Fiordiligi, its sun-changes
Against walls of transparent stone
Unsettling all preconception—a city
For architects (they are taught
By casting their nets
Into those moving shoals); and there is
Kairouan, whose lit space
So slides into and fits
The stone masses, one would doubt
Which was the more solid
Unless, folding back
Gold segments out of the white
Pith globe of a quartered orange,
One may learn perhaps
To read such perspectives. At Luna

There is a city of bridges, where
Even the inhabitants are mindful
Of a shared privilege: a bridge
Does not exist for its own sake.
It commands vacancy.

# At Delft

*(Johannes Vermeer, 1632–75)*

The clocks begin, civicly simultaneous,
    And the day's admitted. It shines to show
How promptness is poverty, unless
    Poetry be the result of it. The chimes
Stumble asunder, intricate and dense,
    Then mass at the hour, their stroke
In turn a reminder: for if one dances
    One does so to a measure. And this
Is a staid but dancing town, each street
    Its neighbour's parallel, each house
A displacement in that mathematic, yet
    Built of a common brick. Within
The key is changed: the variant recurs
    In the invariable tessellation of washed floors,
As cool as the stuffs are warm, as ordered
    As they are opulent. White earthenware,
A salver, stippled at its lip by light,
    The light itself, diffused and indiscriminate
On face and floor, usher us in,
    The guests of objects: as in a landscape,
All that is human here stands clarified
    By all that accompanies and bounds. The clocks
Chime muted underneath domestic calm.

# The Jam Trap

Wings filmed, the threads of knowledge thicken
Corded with mire. Bodies immerse
Slackly in sweetness. Sweetness is not satisfaction
Nor was the elation of the pursuit
The measure of its end. Aromas and inclinations

Delectable essences, and now
The inextricable gesture, sounds
Which communicate nothing, their sole speech
A scurrying murmur, each to himself his own
Monotone burden of discouragement. Preferring
The fed flock that, scattered, re-forms
Massed into echelon above copious fields,
The sky, their chosen element, has abandoned them.

## Poem

Upended, it crouches on broken limbs
About to run forward. No longer threatened
But surprised into this vigilance
It gapes enmity from its hollowed core.

Moist woodflesh, softened to a paste
Of marl and white splinter, dangles
Where overhead the torn root
Casts up its wounds in a ragged orchis.

The seasons strip, but do not tame you.
I grant you become more smooth
As you are emptied and where the heart shreds
The gap mouths a more practised silence.

You would impress, but merely startle. Your accomplice
Twilight is dragging its shadows here
Deliberate and unsocial: I leave you
To your one meaning, yourself alone.

## A Meditation on John Constable

'Painting is a science, and should be pursued as an inquiry into the laws of nature.
Why, then, may not landscape painting be considered as a branch of natural
philosophy, of which pictures are but the experiments?'

(JOHN CONSTABLE, *The History of Landscape Painting*)

He replied to his own question, and with the unmannered
    Exactness of art; enriched his premises
By confirming his practice: the labour of observation
    In face of meteorological fact. Clouds

Followed by others, temper the sun in passing
   Over and off it. Massed darks
Blotting it back, scattered and mellowed shafts
   Break damply out of them, until the source
Unmasks, floods its retreating bank
   With raw fire. One perceives (though scarcely)
The remnant clouds trailing across it
   In rags, and thinned to a gauze.
But the next will dam it. They loom past
   And narrow its blaze. It shrinks to a crescent
Crushed out, a still lengthening ooze
   As the mass thickens, though cannot exclude
Its silvered-yellow. The eclipse is sudden,
   Seen first on the darkening grass, then complete
In a covered sky.
               Facts. And what are they?
He admired accidents, because governed by laws,
   Representing them (since the illusion was not his end)
As governed by feeling. The end is our approval
   Freely accorded, the illusion persuading us
That it exists as a human image. Caught
   By a wavering sun, or under a wind
Which moistening among the outlines of banked foliage
   Prepares to dissolve them, it must grow constant;
Though there, ruffling and parted, the disturbed
   Trees let through the distance, like white fog
Into their broken ranks. It must persuade
   And with a constancy, not to be swept back
To reveal what it half-conceals. Art is itself
   Once we accept it. The day veers. He would have judged
Exactly in such a light, that strides down
   Over the quick stains of cloud-shadows
Expunged now, by its conflagration of colour.
   A descriptive painter? If delight
Describes, which wrings from the brush
   The errors of a mind, so tempered,
It can forgo all pathos; for what he saw
   Discovered what he was, and the hand—unswayed
By the dictation of a single sense—
   Bodied the accurate and total knowledge
In a calligraphy of present pleasure. Art
   Is complete when it is human. It is human
Once the looped pigments, the pin-heads of light
   Securing space under their deft restrictions

Convince, as the index of a possible passion,
    As the adequate gauge, both of the passion
And its object. The artist lies
    For the improvement of truth. Believe him.


# Frondes Agrestes

### On re-reading Ruskin

A leaf, catching the sun, transmits it:
'First a torch, then an emerald.'

'Compact, like one of its own cones':
The round tree with the pyramid shadow.

First the felicities, then
The feelings to appraise them:

Light, being in its untempered state,
A rarity, we are (says the sage) meant
To enjoy 'most probably' the effects of mist.

Nature's difficulties, her thought
Over dints and bosses, her attempts
To beautify with a leopard-skin of moss
The rocks she has already sculpted,
All disclose her purposes—the thrush's bill,
The shark's teeth, are not his story.

Sublimity is. One awaits its passing,
Organ voice dissolving among cloud wrack.
The climber returns. He brings
Sword-shaped, its narrowing strip
Fluted and green, the single grass-blade, or
Gathered up into its own translucence
Where there is no shade save colour, the unsymbolic rose.

# Geneva Restored

'The secreted city'...' F. T. PRINCE

Limestone, faulted with marble; the lengthening swell
Under the terraces, the farms in miniature, until
With its sheer, last leap, the Salève becomes
The Salève, juts naked, the cliff which nobody sees
Because it pretends to be nothing, and has shaken off
Its seashore litter of house-dots. Beneath that,
This—compact, as the other is sudden, and with an inaccessible
Family dignity: close roofs on a gravel height,
Building knit into rock; the bird's nest of a place
Rich in protestant pieties, in heroic half-truths
That was Ruskin's. Guard and rebuild it. We are in the time
(The eternity rather) before the esplanades, New York
Bear-ridden and the casino unbuilt, Paris and London
Remain at Paris and London, and four miles square
A canton of resined air that will not be six
Refreshes a sociality that will not be pent
In the actual. Round this inconceivable
Point of patience, men travel on foot.

# Farewell to Van Gogh

The quiet deepens. You will not persuade
    One leaf of the accomplished, steady, darkening
Chestnut-tower to displace itself
    With more of violence than the air supplies
When, gathering dusk, the pond brims evenly
    And we must be content with stillness.

Unhastening, daylight withdraws from us its shapes
    Into their central calm. Stone by stone
Your rhetoric is dispersed until the earth
    Becomes once more the earth, the leaves
A sharp partition against cooling blue.

Farewell, and for your instructive frenzy
    Gratitude. The world does not end tonight
And the fruit that we shall pick tomorrow
    Await us, weighing the unstripped bough.

# Cézanne at Aix

And the mountain: each day
Immobile like fruit. Unlike, also
—Because irreducible, because
Neither a component of the delicious
And therefore questionable,
Nor distracted (as the sitter)
By his own pose and, therefore,
Doubly to be questioned: it is not
Posed. It is. Untaught
Unalterable, a stone bridgehead
To that which is tangible
Because unfelt before. There
In its weathered weight
Its silence silences, a presence
Which does not present itself.

# In Defence of Metaphysics

Place is the focus. What is the language
Of stones? I do not mean
As emblems of patience, philosophers' hopes
Or as the astrological tangents
One may assemble, draw out subjectively
From a lapidary inertia. Only we
Are inert. Stones act, like pictures, by remaining
Always the same, unmoving, waiting on presence
Unpredictable in absence, inhuman
In a human dependence, a physical
Point of contact, for a movement not physical
And on a track of force, the milestone
Between two infinities. Stones are like deaths.
They uncover limits.

# Reeds

The blades sway. They ride
Unbleached, tugged in their full sap
By the slow current. Hindering

37

From thought, they think us back
To that first green, which the mind
Tender-skinned, since grazed to the pain of sight,
Shrank at, lapping us in a half-green content
And, there, left us. By nature
Trenchant, blue double-whets them,
Burned through the water from a sky
That has long looked at it
Untempered by any mist. In this
There is of theme or apophthegm
No more than meets the eye. The blades sway.

## *The Shell*

A white spire,
Its peak encircled
By a stair, a second
Stair corkscrewed inside it:
Gradually
You absorb all thought
Into that twisted matrix
From which nothing is born;
And like the speaker
Who hesitates to offend
And offends by hesitation
You propose your question
In silence, your hesitancy
The appearance only
Of a fragility whose centre
Is hard. You offend
Because you are there
Like the mountain
Which the too-civil fancy
Cannot appropriate to itself.
Your opalescence
Has seemed beautiful,
But a surface is as beautiful
As that which hides beneath it.
The irony of your finitude
Mirroring our own, we halt
Here where the shadow stains
At its white threshold
Your concealed stair.

# Night-Piece: The Near and the Far

Declivities, striations, ledge over ledge of mounting
Cloud. A solid smoke, unsifted before the wind,
But shaped against it, crowded and blown together
From the horizon upwards. It goes on drifting, piling,
Rags into rock-ranks, mist to masses
Caught endlessly through the alien current, held
Riding the stream which buoys, then bloats, drags it
Into a further dark. Fissured, lit by the moon behind
Prizing from black an ore of undertones,
Over the houseless space, a hearth spills down.

# At Holwell Farm

It is a quality of air, a temperate sharpness
    Causes an autumn fire to burn compact,
To cast from a shapely and unrifted core
    Its steady brightness. A kindred flame
Gathers within the stone, and such a season
    Fosters, then frees it in a single glow:
Pears by the wall and stone as ripe as pears
    Under the shell-hood's cornice; the door's
Bright oak, the windows' slim-cut frames
    Are of an equal whiteness. Crude stone
By a canopy of shell, each complements
    In opposition, each is bound
Into a pattern of utilities—this farm
    Also a house, this house a dwelling.
Rooted in more than earth, to dwell
    Is to discern the Eden image, to grasp
In a given place and guard it well
    Shielded in stone. Whether piety
Be natural, is neither the poet's
    Nor the builder's story, but a quality of air,
Such as surrounds and shapes an autumn fire
    Bringing these sharp disparities to bear.

# On the Hall at Stowey

Walking by map, I chose unwonted ground,
   A crooked, questionable path which led
Beyond the margin, then delivered me
   At a turn. Red marl
Had rutted the aimless track
   That firmly withheld the recompense it hid
Till now, close by its end, the day's discoveries
   Began with the dimming night:

A house. The wall-stones, brown.
   The doubtful light, more of a mist than light
Floating at hedge-height through the sodden fields
   Had yielded, or a final glare
Burst there, rather, to concentrate
   Sharp saffron, as the ebbing year—
Or so it seemed, for the dye deepened—poured
   All of its yellow strength through the way I went:

Over grass, garden-space, over the grange
   That jutted beyond, lengthening-down
The house line, tall as it was,
   By tying it to the earth, trying its pride
(Which submitted) under a nest of barns,
   A walled weight of lesser encumbrances—
Few of which worsened it, and none
   As the iron sheds, sealing my own approach.

All stone. I had passed these last, unwarrantable
   Symbols of—no; let me define, rather
The thing they were not, all that we cannot be,
   By the description, simply of that which merits it:
Stone. Why must (as it does at each turn)
   Each day, the mean rob us of patience, distract us
Before even its opposite?—before stone, which
   Cut, piled, mortared, is patience's presence.

The land farmed, the house was neglected: but
   Gashed panes (and there were many) still showed
Into the pride of that presence. I had reached
   Unchallenged, within feet of the door

Ill-painted, but at no distant date—the least
  Our prodigal time could grudge it; paused
To measure the love, to assess its object,
  That trusts for continuance to the mason's hand.

Five centuries—here were (at the least) five—
  In linked love, eager excrescence
Where the door, arched, crowned with acanthus,
  Aimed at a civil elegance, but hit
This sturdier compromise, neither Greek, Gothic
  Nor Strawberry, clumped from the arching-point
And swathing down, like a fist of wheat,
  The unconscious emblem for the house's worth.

Conclusion surrounded it, and the accumulation
  After Lammas growth. Still coming on
Hart's-tongue by maiden-hair
  Thickened beneath the hedges, the corn levelled
And carried, long-since; but the earth
  (Its tint glowed in the house wall)
Out of the reddish dark still thrust up foison
  Through the browning-back of the exhausted year:

Thrust through the unweeded yard, where earth and house
  Debated the terrain. My eye
Caught in those flags a gravestone's fragment
  Set by a careful century. The washed inscription
Still keen, showed only a fragile stem
  A stave, a broken circlet, as
(Unintelligibly clear, craft in the sharp decrepitude)
  A pothook grooved its firm memorial.

Within, wet from the failing roof,
  Walls greened. Each hearth refitted
For a suburban whim, each room
  Denied what it was, diminished thus
To a barbarous mean, had comforted (but for a time)
  Its latest tenant. Angered, I turned to my path
Through the inhuman light, light that a fish might swim
  Stained by the greyness of the smoking fields.

Five centuries. And we? What we had not
  Made ugly, we had laid waste—
Left (I should say) the office to nature

Whose blind battery, best fitted to perform it
Outdoes us, completes by persistence
   All that our negligence fails in. Saddened,
Yet angered beyond sadness, where the road
   Doubled upon itself I halted, for a moment
Facing the empty house and its laden barns.


# *Stone Walls: at Chew Magna*

In this unyielding, even
Afternoon glow
One by one
You could unfasten
Like the tendrils of ivy
The filaments of all these
Sagging networks
Where the shadowed space
Divides walls
Into friable pink blocks
And the glow would spread
More evenly over
Their resolved opacity,
But who would unmake
This dislocation where
Each is located?


# *Cradock Newton: From an Epitaph*

'Gurney, Hampton, Cradock Newton, last
Held on the measure of that antient line
Of barons' blood . . .' Paused by whose tomb,
Ignorant of its bones I read the claim
(Lie, half-lie or three-quarters true): 'He lov'd
To feed the poor.' Tasting such phrases,
So I taste their plight, and pity them,
But seeing the angel with its scales of stone—

Who suffers (I ask in thought) the greater need
Now time has stripped them both—those nameless
Or these named? For pity is the most
That love dares plead from justice. And will the poor
Love Cradock Newton when he creeps unhoused,
Naked at last before the rich man's door?


## *The Castle*

It is a real one—no more symbolic
Than you or I. There are no secrets
Concerning the castellan; in the afternoons
His hospitality labours for the satisfaction
Not of guests, but visitors; in the mornings
Directing his renovations, he sits alone;
A settled gloom is threaded by scavengers
Who, through the dust of galleries, down
Through those sadder reticulations from which the myths have faded,
Resurrect for the present as much of the improbable past
As it can tolerate. Dust is their element
But they finger the mysteries, as they unlink
The pendants of chandeliers into their winking suds:
He is easeless watching this progress, they
Sullen among their swaying burdens, remain
Unmindful of the minuter jealousies he would haunt them with
But which (since his power is nominal)
He must mute into reprimands, or twist, unnoticed
Round the stem of a candle-sconce, to suffer in person
Those daily burnishings under a menial hand.
He looks away. Townwards, below him
Where the sidings smoke, his glance struggles
Then settles. He has risen by the scale of talent
Into the seat of blood. But justice is less than just
And he is bored. His own master and his prisoner,
He serves a public. The soot sifts through
In flocculent grains and the clouds he watches
He now tastes. Whom does a public serve?
The smoke unwinds from its mounting coils,
Falling apart, a wavering drift
As the wind takes it. This morning blur
Conceals no innuendoes. A statement in prose,

It reserves on its neighbouring hill
A last artifact which, dusted, is ready now
To receive the solemnity or the distraction
Of visitors. He rises to go down.
It is twelve, and conscience excuses him.

## Sconset

I have never been
To Sconset, but the gleam
Of painted houses
Adding a snow-tone
To the sea-tone in the mind's
Folder of the principal views
With the courthouse
Seen from the harbour, the harbour
Obscured by the whiteness
Of the church, crouched
Behind a dark shrub
Whose serrated leaves
Hang mounted (as it were)
On the spine of a feather—
These have invaded
All I shall ever hear
To their contrary.

## Civilities of Lamplight

Without excess (no galaxies
Gauds, illiterate exclamations)
It betokens haven,
An ordering, the darkness held
But not dismissed. One man
Alone with his single light
Wading obscurity refines the instance,
Hollows the hedge-bound track, a sealed
Furrow on dark, closing behind him.

# Fire in a Dark Landscape

And where it falls, a quality
Not of the night, but of the mind
As when, on the moonlit roofs,
A counterfeit snow
Whitely deceives us. And yet . . .
It is the meeting, of light
With dark, challenges the memory
To reveal itself, in an unfamiliar form,
As here: red branches
Into a transparency
In liquid motion, the winds'
Chimera of silk, twisting
Thickened with amber shadows,
A quality, not of the mind
But of fire on darkness.

# The Request

Look from your stillness as the light resumes.
  From underneath your brim that, shading,
Sags like a burdock leaf, review
  Once more the accretions of moss
Greying the stones at the level of your eye.

Recover, rising, the ease in which you came
  Spreading on the grass your scarf and then yourself
Laid on its crimson that would have challenged
  Till you offset it, leaning there
With the unconscious rectitude of grace
  A little stiffly upon the elbow. Recall

Gradually the supple line
  With which your hand, composing the calm
You and your solitary companion share,
  Dipped, reiterated the brim in undulation,
Then subsided as you removed your elbow
  To slide instantly into that present shade.

She looks. And a flawed perfection
   Disburses her riches. She is watched
And knows she is watched. The crimson reveals itself
   Recommending her posture and assured by it
Both of her charm and her complicity: the error
   And the request were mine, the conclusion is yours.


## Château de Muzot

Than a choice of subject,
Rather to be chosen by what has to be said
And to say it—by cold fire
Such as these walls withhold and the eye
Tactually commends, the light
Thereby assuring us of a mass
That we would wish to touch. From this
You cannot detract. It is beyond satire
And beyond you. A shriven self
Looks out at it. You cannot
Add to this. Footholds for foison
There are none. Across stoneface
Only the moss, flattened, tightly-rosetted
Which, ignorant of who gives
Accepts from all weathers
What it receives, possessed
By the nature of stone.


## The Ruin

Dissolving, the coals shift. Rain swaddles us
   And the fire, driving its shadows through the room
Recalls us to our intention as the flames
   That, by turns, sink guttering or mount
To pour red light through every crater,
   Threaten the galleries of crumbling ash.

The ruins sag, then sift downwards,
   Their fall so soundless that, for the first time,
We distinguish the unbroken, muffled sibilance
   Rain has accompanied us with. Our talk
Recovers its theme—the ruin we should have visited
   Abandoned, now, in its own emptiness.

For the morning promised what, through the darkening air,
   Afternoon retracted, nor will the evening
Welcome us under its turmoil of wet leaves
   Where we have lost the keenness of such acridity
As a burnt ruin exhales long afterwards
   Into the coolness when rain has ceased.

It stands on the hill slope. Between green and green
   There is the boundary wall that circles
And now hides it. Within, one can see nothing
   Save the third, chequered indefinite green
Of treetops—until, skirting these limits
   One discovers, open upon the emptied confine, the gate.

For a week, the swift traffic of demolition
   That mottled with oil their stagnant rain,
Advanced through the deepening ruts,
   Converged on the house, disjointed, reassembled
And carted, flung (what had sprawled unhinged)
   The door into the wreckage and burnt both.

The door which, though elegant, leaned from the true
   A little to one side, was shamed
By the nearby, slender but rigid elm—
   An unchanging comedy, varied
Only as the seasons thought fit and as the days
   Under their shifting lights reviewed it.

The house was not ancient, but old: deserted,
   The slewed door had focused its rotting style
And, as proportion tugged from decrepitude
   A faint self-respect, it was the door
With the firmness of an aged but practised arbiter
   Bestowed it back over the entire ruin.

Impartial with imperfections, it could accuse
    By this scant presence its clustering neighbours
Gross with the poverty of utility. Thus challenging, it stayed,
    A problem for the authorities, a retreat for urchins
Until the urchins burnt half and the authorities
    Publicly accomplished what their ally had attempted by stealth.

There remains now the levelled parapet of earth,
    The bleak diagram of a foundation, a hearth
Focusing nothing and, cast into it, the filigree ghost
    Of an iron fanlight. Could we assemble
Beside its other fragments, that last grace
    Under this meaner roof, they would accuse us still—

And accusing, speak from beyond their dereliction
    Out of their life; as when a vase
Cracked into shards, would seem
    Baldly to confess, 'Men were here',
The arabesque reproves it, tracing in faint lines:
    'Ceremonies and order were here also.'

Nor could we answer: our houses
    Are no longer ourselves; they dare not
Enter our hopes as the guests of meditation
    To reanimate, warmed by this contact,
The laric world where the bowl glistens with presence
    Gracing the table on which it unfolds itself.

Thus fire, renewed at our hearth, consumes.
    Yet it cannot create from the squalor of moderation
A more than fortuitous glory, multiplying its image
    Over the projections of lacquered wood. Charged with their past,
Those relics smoulder before they are compounded
    And turned by the spade under a final neatness.

The window lightens. The shell parts
    Beyond between cloud and sky line.
Thunder-light, flushing the walls, yellows them
    Into a more ardent substance than their own
And can do no more. The effect is nature's
    Who ignores it, and in whose impoverishment we domicile.

# Aqueduct

Let it stand
A stone guest
In an unhospitable land,
Its speech, the well's speech,
The unsealed source's,
Carrying thence
Its own sustenance. Its grace
Must be the match
Of the stream's strength,
And let the tone
Of the waters' flute
Brim with its gentle admonitions the conduit stone.


# Encounter

Birdless, the bush yet shakes
With a bird's alighting. Fate
Is transmitting flight
That rootwards flows,
Each unstilled spray
Tense like a dense arrival of targeted arrows.

---


# ANTECEDENTS

## A Homage and Valediction

'Oh! que ses yeux ne parlent plus d'Idéal
Mais simplement d'humains échanges!'

'After such knowledge, what forgiveness?'

### The scene
Chiefly the Paris of Jules Laforgue and
Stéphane Mallarmé

# I. Nothing: a Divagation

Not the calm—the clarity
After the storm. There are
In lucidity itself
Its crystal abysses
Perspective within perspective:
The white mind holds
An insufficiency, a style
To contain a solitude
And nothing more. Thus,
The infirm alchemy
Of platonic fantasy—
Word, the idea,
Spacing the vacuum: snow-prints
Wanting a direction; perhaps
At the most, as a constellation
The cut stone
Reassembled on dark.


# II. Praeludium

'Je ne puis quitter ce ton: que d'échos...'
                        DERNIERS VERS

The horn has sounded.

Sunsets! They are interminable. Too late, however
For his exclamations. Sunsets ... A point
Of interrogation, perhaps? How long
Can a sun go on setting? The thin refrain
Dies in a dying light as
'The splendour falls.' And it continues
Falling flaking into the leaf-drift. First,
It was Byron; the laureate
Next remarked on the inveterate music
Microscopically, reserving his
Tintinnabulations (caught in the half-stopped ear)
For elegiacs between occasions, the slow sun
Maintaining its progress (downwards)
Chromatically lamented. 'He is a master

Of miniature,' said Nietzsche
Speaking from solitude
Into solitude—he was describing
The bayreuthian minotaur, lamenting the hecatombs,
Yet forced to concede
An undionysiac, unapollonian distinction
In that gamut of melancholias. 'Art is a keyboard
For transitions,' said Mallarmé: 'between something and nothing.'
The music persisted
'And when I heard it' (Charles Baudelaire, the
Slow horn pouring through dusk an orange twilight)
'I grew insatiate.' We had our laureates, they
Their full orchestra and its various music. To that
                                                        Enter
On an ice-drift
A white bear, the grand Chancellor
From Analyse, uncertain
Of whom he should bow to, or whether
No one is present. It started with Byron, and
Liszt, says Heine, bowed to the ladies. But Jules . . .
Outside,

   De la musique avant toute chose
The thin horns gone glacial
And behind blinds, partitioning Paris
Into the rose-stained mist,
He bows to the looking-glass. Sunsets.


# III. Lacunae

    Autumn! Leaves in symphonic tumult,
    Fall of Antigones and Philomelas
    That my grave-digger (alas, poor Yorick!)
    Must shift with his spade; and from the window
    In the wet, all my chimneys
    On the factories . . .

    Chaplin, as Hamlet. A role we have yet to see
    For the most part. As also
    That spoiled Lutheran, masked
    As his Zarathustra. Our innate
    Perspicacity for the moderate

51

Is a national armoury. 'I have not
Read him; I have read about him':
In usum delphini—for the use
Of the common man. After Nietzsche
(Downwards) Sartre, after whom
Anouilh, dauphin's delight. And thus
Rimbaud the incendiary,
Gamin contemporary
With Gosse, the gentleman
Arrived late. He was dressed
In the skin of a Welsh lion, or the lion
Wore his—for the light
Was dubious, the marsh softening
And the company, willing to be led
Back to the forsaken garden by a route
Unfamiliar—yet as it wound
Dimly among the fetishes, a bewilderment
Of reminiscence. The force
That through the green dark, drove them
Muffled dissatisfactions. Last light, low among tempests
Of restless brass. Last music
For the sable throne (She comes, she comes!)
As the horns, one by one
Extinguish under the wave
Rising into the level darkness.
                                And Chaplin,
As Hamlet? That would have been
A more instructive frenzy. Eye-level light
Disclosing the field's wrinkles
Closes.


# IV. Milieux

              We lack nothing
But the milieu.
                    De la fumée avant toute chose
Weaving the smoke, subjective
Faun with a cigarette Stéphane assembled one:
The page (the horns gone glacial)
Discovered its landscapes
As arctic gardens,
A luminous aura, hinting the penetration

Of green skeins, a snow-light
Bruising the mind.

                There were divagations (platonic)
There were departures (actual)
And the predilection
For a confirmed madness
Confused them, one with another. Thus Missolonghi
Was re-enacted at Harrar
At Papeete, Atouana—'alone
And surrounded by verdure':
Preludes to Taos.

                We lack nothing
But a significant sun.


# V. The Bells: A Period Piece

'What a world of solemn thought ...' POE

Hygienic bells, pale
Galilean bells (O what a wealth
Of melody!)—the lingering
Aftertone of all that sullen, moneyed harmony
Drove, and will drive, before its tidal choir
The great departures and the soft refusals.

Expostulation with the deaf—impossible
'To modify this situation':
Rustle of lavender and thyme, clean collars
As the wind is gagged
Full of this crystalline confusion:

The sky, dressed in the sound of Sunday colours
The season (fall of Antigones and Philomelas!)
The trains (picturesque destinations!) missed
The girls (white as their prayer-books) are released,
Rustle in lavender and thyme
From incense back to houses where
Their white pianos cool each thirsty square.

Chimeric bells, provincial bells—
And from the rust within their throats (O what a world
Of solemn thought!) now silence breaks:
Secure no longer in their theme
Or violence of its repetitions,
The generations abdicate
To us the means to vacillate.

## VI. Something: A Direction

Out of the shut cell of that solitude there is
　　One egress, past point of interrogation.
Sun is, because it is not you; you are
　　Since you are self, and self delimited
Regarding sun. It downs? I claim? Cannot
　　Beyond such speech as this, gather conviction?
Judge, as you will, not what I say
　　But what is, being said. It downs
Recovered, coverless, in a shriven light
　　And you, returning, may to a shriven self
As from the scene, your self withdraws. You are downing
　　Back from that autumn music of the light, which
Split by your need, to know the textures of your pain,
　　Refuses them in your acceptance. You accept
An evening, washed of its overtones
　　By strict seclusion, yet are not secluded
Withheld at your proper bounds. From there
　　Your returns may enter, welcome strangers
Into a civil country (you were not the first
　　To see it), but a country, natural and profuse
Unbroken by past incursions, as the theme
　　Strung over stave, is rediscovered
After dismemberment in the canon, and over stave
　　Can still proceed, unwound, unwinding
To its established presence, its territory
　　Staked and sung; and the phrase descends
As a phase concluded. Released
　　From knowing to acknowledgement, from prison
To powers, you are new-found
　　Neighboured, having earned relation
With all that is other. Still you must wait,
　　For evening's ashen, like the slow fire

54

Withdrawn through the whitened log
   Glinting through grain marks where the wood splits:
Let be its being: the scene extends
   Not hope, but the urgency that hopes for means.


## Notes to Antecedents

III. *Lacunae*

'The force/That through the green dark . . .'
(Cf. DYLAN THOMAS, *Eighteen Poems*.)

IV. *Milieux*

Rimbaud departed to Harrar; Gauguin to Papeete and Atouana. From Atouana
the latter wrote: 'You have no idea of the peace in which I live here, entirely
alone, surrounded by verdure.' (Quoted by R. H. WILENSKI, p. 177, *Modern French
Painters*, Faber 1944.)

V. *The Bells*

'Impossible de modifier cette situation.' In rendering this from *Derniers Vers*, one
cannot avoid the tone of (early) Eliot because Eliot himself has not avoided the
tone of Laforgue.


## The Churchyard Wall

Stone against stone, they are building back
   Round the steepled bulk, a wall
That enclosed from the neighbouring road
   The silent community of graves. James Bridle,
Jonathan Silk and Adam Bliss, you are well housed
   Dead, howsoever you lived—such headstones
Lettered and scrolled, and such a wall
   To repel the wind. The channel, first,
Dug to contain a base in solid earth
   And filled with the weightier fragments. The propped yews
Will scarcely outlast it; for, breached,
   It may be rebuilt. The graves weather
And the stone skulls, more ruinous
   Than art had made them, fade by their broken scrolls.
It protects the dead. The living regard it
   Once it is falling, and for the rest

55

Accept it. Again, the ivy
  Will clasp it down, save for the buried base
And that, where the frost has cracked,
  Must be trimmed, reset, and across its course
The barrier raised. Now they no longer
  Prepare: they build, judged by the dead.
The shales must fit, the skins of the wall-face
  Flush, but the rising stones
Sloped to the centre, balanced upon an incline.
They work at ease, the shade drawn in
To the uncoped wall which casts it, unmindful
  For the moment, that they will be outlasted
By what they create, that their labour
  Must be undone. East and west
They cope it edgewise; to the south
  Where the talkers sit, taking its sun
When the sun has left it, they have lain
  The flat slabs that had fallen inwards
Mined by the ivy. They leave completed
  Their intent and useful labours to be ignored,
To pass into common life, a particle
  Of the unacknowledged sustenance of the eye,
Less serviceable than a house, but in a world of houses
  A merciful structure. The wall awaits decay.


## *Epitaph*

Enamoured by
Brevity in method,
'The unlettered muse'
Now outdoes
Her favourite
Device of rhetoric—
Namely, the pretence
Of having none.
Wordsworth admired
The named and dated
Day-old child, of her
Who alike conceived
This dateless
And initialled grave.

# A PEOPLED LANDSCAPE
## (1963)

*I want the cries of my geese to echo in
space.*

JEAN-FRANÇOIS MILLET

# A Prelude

I want the cries of my geese
To echo in space, and the land
They fly above to be astir beneath
The agreement of its forms, as if it were
A self one might inhabit: life
Under leaf, gulls going in
Behind the encroachment of the plough.
Futurity, now open-handedly
Leans to the present and the season
Re-establishes a reign of outwardness,
Begins to build the summer back in cries
Still haunted by the cold, as geese
Cross over skies where mid-March balances.

# Return to Hinton

*Written on the author's return to Hinton Blewett from the United States*

Ten years
   and will you be
      a footnote, merely,
England
   of the Bible
      open at Genesis
on the parlour table?
   'God
      saw the light
that it was good.'
   It falls
      athwart the book
through window-lace
   whose shadow
      decorates the sheets
of 'The Bridal March'—
   a square of white
      above the keyboard
and below
   a text which is a prayer.
      The television box
is one,

the mullions and flagged floor
of the kitchen
through an open door
witness a second
world in which
beside the hob
the enormous kettles'
blackened bellies ride—
as much the tokens of an order as
the burnished brass.
You live
between the two
and, ballasted against
the merely new, the tide
and shift of time
you wear
your widow's silk
your hair
plaited, as it has been
throughout those years
whose rime it bears.
A tractor
mounts the ramp of stones
into the yard:
a son surveys
the scenes
that occupied a father's days.
Proud of his machine,
will he transmit
that more than bread
that leaves you undisquieted?
This house
is poorer by a death
than last I saw it
yet
who may judge
as poverty that
sadness without bitterness
those sudden tears
that your composure
clears, admonishes?
Your qualities
are like the land
—inherited:

but you
        have earned
                your right to them
have given
        grief its due
                and, on despair,
have closed your door
        as the gravestones tell you to.
                Speak
your composure and you share
        the accent of their rhymes
                express
won readiness
        in a worn dress
                of chapel gospel.
Death's
        not the enemy
                of you nor of your kind:
a surer death
        creeps after me
                out of that generous
rich and nervous land
        where, buried by
                the soft oppression of prosperity
locality's mere grist
        to build
                the even bed
of roads that will not rest
        until they lead
                into a common future
rational
        and secure
                that we must speed
by means that are not either.
        Narrow
                your farm-bred certainties
I do not hold:
        I share
                your certain enemy.
For we who write
        the verse you do not read
                already plead your cause

before
 that cold tribunal
  while you're unaware
they hold their session.
  Our language is our land
   that we'll
not waste or sell
 against a promised mess
  of pottage that we may not taste.
For who has known
 the seasons' sweet succession
  and would still
exchange them for a whim, a wish
 or swim into
  a mill-race for an unglimpsed fish?

## *Winter-Piece*

You wake, all windows blind—embattled sprays
grained on the medieval glass.
Gates snap like gunshot
as you handle them. Five-barred fragility
sets flying fifteen rooks who go together
silently ravenous above this winter-piece
that will not feed them. They alight
beyond, scavenging, missing everything
but the bladed atmosphere, the white resistance.
Ruts with iron flanges track
through a hard decay
where you discern once more
oak-leaf by hawthorn, for the frost
rewhets their edges. In a perfect web
blanched along each spoke
and circle of its woven wheel,
the spider hangs, grasp unbroken
and death-masked in cold. Returning
you see the house glint-out behind
its holed and ragged glaze,
frost-fronds all streaming.

# History

It is the unregarded congruence:
The boy who cries 'Bull'
Because he is leading one
Past the antique cart
Which the winter's advent
Will convert to firewood.
He does not mark it
Nor will he mark its absence—
Himself, the guardian
Of a continuity he cannot see
And—grant him means—
Would injure readily:
Admire, but not revere
This inarticulate philosopher.

# Lines

You have seen a plough
the way it goes breeds
furrows line on line
until they fill a field?

What I admire in this
is less the page complete
and all the insatiable
activity towards it

than when, one furrow
more lies done with
and the tractor hesitates:
another line to be begun

and then it turns and drags
the blade in tow and that
turns too along the new
and growing groove

and each reversal thus
in mitigating mere aggression
prepares for the concerted
on-rush of the operation

and then the dark the cool
the dew corroding the intent
abandoned mechanism
that contemplates accomplishment.

# *Canal*

Swans. I watch them
come unsteadying
the dusty, green
and curving arm
of water. Sinuously
both the live
bird and the bird
the water bends
into a white and wandering
reflection of itself,
go by in grace
a world of objects.
Symmetrically punched
now empty rivet-
holes betray
a sleeper fence:
below its raggedness
the waters darken
and above it rear
the saw-toothed houses
which the swinging
of the waters makes
scarcely less regular
in repetition. Swans
are backed by these, as
these are by
a sky of silhouettes,
all black and almost
all, indefinite.
A whitish smoke

in drifting diagonals
accents, divides
the predominance of street
and chimney lines,
where all is either
mathematically supine
or vertical, except
the pyramids of slag.
And, there, unseen
among such angularities—
a church, a black
freestanding witness
that a space of graves
invisibly is also
there. Only
its clock identifies
the tower between
the accompaniment of stacks
where everything
repeats itself—
the slag, the streets
and water that repeats
them all again
and spreads them rippling
out beneath
the eye of the discriminating
swans that seek
for something else
and the blank brink
concludes them without conclusion.


## *John Maydew* or *The Allotment*

Ranges
        of clinker heaps
                go orange now:
through cooler air
        an acrid drift
                seeps upwards
from the valley mills;
        the spoiled and staled
                distances invade

these closer comities
        of vegetable shade,
                glass-houses, rows
and trellises of red-
        ly flowering beans.
                This
is a paradise
        where you may smell
                the cinders
of quotidian hell beneath you;
        here grow
                their green reprieves
for those
        who labour, linger in
                their watch-chained waistcoats
rolled-back sleeves—
        the ineradicable
                peasant in the dispossessed
and half-tamed Englishman.
        By day, he makes
                a burrow of necessity
from which
        at evening, he emerges
                here.
A thoughtful yet unthinking man,
        John Maydew,
                memory stagnates
in you and breeds
        a bitterness; it grew
                and rooted in your silence
from the day
        you came
                unwitting out of war
in all the pride
        of ribbons and a scar
                to forty years
of mean amends ...
        He squats
                within his shadow
and a toad
        that takes
                into a slack and twitching jaw
the worms he proffers it,
        looks up at him

through eyes that are
as dimly faithless
    as the going years.
        For, once returned
he found that he
    must choose between
        an England, profitlessly green
and this—
    a seamed and lunar grey
        where slag in lavafolds
unrolls beneath him.
    The valley gazes up
        through kindling eyes
as, unregarded at his back
    its hollows deepen
        with the black, extending shadows
and the sounds of day
    explore its coming cavities,
        the night's
refreshed recesses.
    Tomorrow
        he must feed its will,
his interrupted pastoral
    take heart into
        those close
and gritty certainties that lie
    a glowing ruse
        all washed in hesitations now.
He eyes the toad
    beating
        in the assuagement
of his truce.

# Steel

### the night shift

Slung from the gantries cranes
patrol in air and parry
lights the furnaces fling up at them.
Clamour is deepest in the den beneath,
fire fiercest at the frontier where
an arm of water doubles

and disjoints it. There is a principle, a pulse
in all these molten and metallic contraries,
this sweat unseen. For men
facelessly habituated to the glare
outstare it, guide the girders
from their high and iron balconies
and keep the simmering slag-trucks
feeding heap on heap
in regular, successive, sea-on-shore
concussive bursts of dry
and falling sound. And time
is all this measured voice would seem
to ask, until it uncreate
the height and fabric of the light-
lunged, restive, flame-eroded night.


## Crow

The inspecting eye
shows cold
amid the head's
disquieted iridescence.
The whole bird sits
rocking at a vantage
clumsily. The glance
alone is steady
and a will behind it
rights the stance,
corrects all disposition
to ungainly action.
Acting, it will be
as faultless as its eye
in a concerted drop
on carrion; or watch
it fly—the insolence
transfers to wing-tip
and the action wears
an ease that's merciless,
all black assumption,
mounting litheness.
The blown bird,
inaccessible its intimations

of the wind, 'Stay
where you are' is
what it says and we
poor swimmers
in that element
stay, to bear
with clumsy eye
affronted witness at its ways in air.

## Walking to Bells

The spray of sound
(Its echo rides
As bodied as metal
Whose echoes'
Echo it is)
Stunned, released
Where the house-walls
Stand or cease
Blows, or does not
Into the unfilled space
Accordingly; which
Space whose Adam wits
Slept on till now,
Kindles from cold
To hold the entire
Undoubling wave
Distinct in its jewelled collapse,
And the undertone
Sterner and broader than such facile beads
Gainsays
Not one from the toppling hoard its tensed back heaves.

## Portrait of Mrs. Spaxton

No hawk at wrist, but blessed by sudden sun
    And with a single, flaring hen that tops the chair
Blooming beside her where she knits. Before the door
    And in the rainsoaked air, she sits as leisurely
As spaces are with hillshapes in them. Yet she is small—

If she arrests the scene, it is her concentration
That commands it, the three centuries and more
    That live in her, the eyes that frown against the sun
Yet leave intact the features' kindliness, the anonymous
    Composure of the settled act. Sufficient to her day
Is her day's good, and her sufficiency's the refutation
    Of that future where there'll be what there already is—
Prosperity and ennui, and none without the privilege
    To enjoy them both. But let it know
Then what she is now, and when she must
    Lie by the Norman tower, on her stone
Let them engrave the abiding image of her afternoon.


## The Farmer's Wife: at Fostons Ash

Scent
        from the apple-loft!
                I smelt it and I saw
in thought
        behind the oak
                that cupboards all your wine
the store in maturation
        webbed
                and waiting.
There
        we paused in talk,
                the labyrinth of lofts
above us and the stair
        beneath, bound
                for a labyrinth of cellars.
Everywhere
        as darkness
                leaned and loomed
the light was crossing it
        or travelled through
                the doors you opened
into rooms that view
        your hens and herds,
                your cider-orchard.

Proud
you were
displaying these
inheritances
to an eye
as pleased as yours
and as familiar almost
with them. Mine
had known,
had grown into the ways
that regulate such riches
and had seen
your husband's mother's day
and you had done
no violence to that recollection,
proving it
by present fact.
Distrust
that poet who must symbolize
your stair into
an analogue
of what was never there.
Fact
has its proper plenitude
that only time and tact
will show, renew.
It is enough
those steps should be
no more than what they were, that your
hospitable table
overlook the cowshed.
A just geography
completes itself
with such relations, where
beauty and stability can be
each other's equal.
But building is
a biding also
and I saw
one lack
among your store of blessings.
You had come
late into marriage
and your childlessness

was palpable
as we surveyed
            the kitchen, where four unheraldic
                    sheep-dogs kept the floor
and seemed to want
            their complement of children.
                    Not desolateness
changed the scene I left,
            the house
                    manning its hill,
the gabled bulk
            still riding there
                    as though it could
command the crops
            upwards
                    out of willing land;
and yet
            it was as if
            a doubt
within my mood
            troubled the rock of its ancestral certitude.


# The Death of Elizabeth Grieve

*Anno 1958*


Beside the fall, the moonlight spills
    Unseasonable frost. She watches
Zone by zone, the current slide
    Into the moon and stretch, the shafts of water
Sounding for a ground they cannot find—
    Then, powerless, this swinging power
Twist, swept-out in wilder need
    That enters her in its unravelling abandonment
To air, till all she is must fall
    In flight before the moonlight's importunities.

# The Hand at Callow Hill Farm

Silence. The man defined
The quality, ate at his separate table
Silent, not because silence was enjoined
But was his nature. It shut him round
Even at outdoor tasks, his speech
Following upon a pause, as though
A hesitance to comply had checked it—
Yet comply he did, and willingly:
Pause and silence: both
Were essential graces, a reticence
Of the blood, whose calm concealed
The tutelary of that upland field.

# Harvest Festival: at Ozleworth

Here, Romans owned the need—to give
   The giver gifts. I saw again
The shadow of the old propitiation
   In this ritual of preparing: women
Deft amid that fruit, those blooms
   Were priestesses at hecatombs of pear and apple,
Building their banks of leaves beneath
   Leaved capitals. The chancel arch
Seemed like the chosen counter-bass
   To show the theme weaving about it. There
Thorns were the crown to all the fruits: the hand
   That faultlessly had spanned the space, had cut
For a crossing in the stone, the spines
   Which Christ had worn, long lobes
In interlacing, shadowed grey. Cruel, these
   Cool fingers, tip to tip, and yet
Whoever wove them had not lost delight
   In the conception. Though they stood for more
Than we could ever be or bear, they fed
   The eye with regularity, humanized the hurt.
This, growing kind, could thus
   Remind us of the necessary pain that none

Is proof against, and even stone
    Must neighbour. The garlands took the theme
Back to delight again, to gratitude,
    Scent, earth and (since the season
Brings in death) delight and death
    Ran in this canon graced to sanctify
Ceres with the chastened music of our festivity.

## The Picture of J. T. in a Prospect of Stone

What should one
    wish a child
        and that, one's own
emerging
    from between
        the stone lips
of a sheep-stile
    that divides
        village graves
and village green?
    —Wish her
        the constancy of stone.
—But stone
    is hard.
        —Say, rather
it resists
    the slow corrosives
        and the flight
of time
    and yet it takes
        the play, the fluency
from light.
    —How would you know
        the gift you'd give
was the gift
    she'd wish to have?
        —Gift is giving,
gift is meaning:
    first
        I'd give
then let her
    live with it

74

to prove
its quality the better and
thus learn
to love
what (to begin with)
she might spurn.
—You'd
moralize a gift?
—I'd have her
understand
the gift I gave her.
—And so she shall
but let her play
her innocence away
emerging
as she does
between
her doom (unknown),
her unmown green.


# The Chestnut Avenue: at Alton House

Beneath their flames, cities of candelabra
    Gathering-in a more than civic dark
Sway between green and gloom,
    Prepare a way of hushed submergence
Where the eye descries no human house,
    But a green trajectory in whose depths
Glimmers a barrier of stone. At the wind's invasion
    The greenness teeters till the indented parallels
Lunge to a restive halt, defying still
    The patient geometry that planted them
Thus, in their swaying stations. We have lent them
    Order—they, greeting that gift
With these incalculable returns. Mindless
    They lead the mind its ways, deny
The imposition of its frontiers, as the wind, their ally,
    Assails the civility of the façade they hide
Their green indifference barbarous at its panes.

# Four Kantian Lyrics

*for Paul Roubiczek*

## 1. *On a Theme of Pasternak*

I stared, but not to seize
the point of things: it was an incidental
sharpness held me there,
watching a sea of leaves
put out the sun. Spark
by spark, they drew it slowly down
sifting the hoard in glints
and pinheads. Rents of space
threatened to let it through
but, no—at once, the same
necessity that tamed the sky
to a single burning tone
would drag it deeper. Light
was suddenly beneath the mass
and silhouette of skirts and fringes,
shrinking to a glow on grass.
With dark, a breeze comes in
sends staggering the branches'
blackened ledges till they rear
recoiling. And now the trees are there
no longer, one can hear it climb
repeatedly their sullen hill
of leaves, rake and rouse them,
then their gathered tide
set floating all the house on air.

## 2. *What it was like*

It was like the approach of flame
treading the tinder, a fleet
cascade of it taking tree-toll,
halting below the hill and then
covering the corn-field's dryness
in an effortless crescendo. One heard
in the pause of the receding silence
the whole house grow
tense through its ties, the beams
brace beneath pantiles
for the coming burst. It came

76

and went. The blinded pane
emerged from the rainsheet
to an after-water world,
its green confusion brought
closer greener. The baptism
of the shining house was done
and it was like the calm
a church aisle harbours
tasting of incense, space and stone.

### 3. *An Insufficiency of Earth*

The wind goes over it. You see
the broken leaf-cope breathe
subsidingly, and lift itself
like water levelling. Stemmed,
this cloud of green, this mammoth
full of detail shifts
its shimmering, archaic head
no more. You think it for a second
hugely dead, until the ripple
soundless on the further corn,
is roaring in it. We cannot pitch
our paradise in such a changeful
nameless place and our encounters
with it. An insufficiency of earth
denies our constancy. For,
content with the iridescence of the moment,
we must flow with the wood-fleece
in a war of forms, the wind
gone over us, and we
drinking its imprints, faceless as the sea.

### 4. *How it happened*

It happened like this: I heard
from the farm beyond, a grounded
churn go down. The sound
chimed for the wedding of the mind
with what one could not see,
the further fields, the seamless
spread of space, and then,
all bestial ease, the cows
foregathered by the milking place
in a placid stupor. There are two

ways to marry with a land—
first, this bland and blind
submergence of the self, an act
of kind and questionless. The other
is the thing I mean, a whole
event, a happening, the sound
that brings all space in
for its bound, when self is clear
as what we keenest see and hear:
no absolute of eye can tell
the utmost, but the glance
goes shafted from us like a well.


## Up at La Serra

The shadow
        ran before it lengthening
                and a wave went over.
Distance
        did not obscure
                the machine of nature:
you could watch it
        squander and recompose itself
                all day, the shadow-run
the sway of the necessity down there
        at the cliff-base
                crushing white from blue.
Come in
        by the arch
                under the campanile parrocchiale
and the exasperation of the water
        followed you,
                its *Soldi, soldi*
unpicking the hill-top peace
        insistently.
                He knew, at twenty
all the deprivations such a place
        stored for the man
                who had no more to offer
than a sheaf of verse
        in the style of Quasimodo.
                Came the moment,

78

he would tell it
         in a poem
                   without rancour, a lucid
testament above his name
         *Paolo*
                   *Bertolani*
—*Ciao, Paolo!*
         —*Ciao*
                   *Giorgino!*
He would put them
         all in it—
                   Giorgino going
over the hill
         to look for labour;
                   the grinder
of knives and scissors
         waiting to come up, until
                   someone would hoist his wheel
on to a back, already
         hooped to take it,
                   so you thought
the weight must crack
         curvature. And then:
                   Beppino and Beppino
friends
         who had in common
                   nothing except their names and friendship;
and the sister of the one
         who played the accordion
                   and under all
the *Soldi, soldi,*
         *sacra conversazione*
                   *del mare—*
*della madre.*
         Sometimes
                   the men had an air of stupefaction:
*La Madre:*
         it was the women there
                   won in a truceless enmity.
At home
         a sepia-green
                   *Madonna di Foligno*
shared the wall

with the October calendar—
Lenin looked out of it,
Mao
blessing the tractors
and you told
the visitors:
*We are not communists*
*although we call ourselves communists*
*we are what you English*
*would call ... socialists.*
He believed
that God was a hypothesis,
that the party would bring in
a synthesis, that he
would edit the local paper for them,
or perhaps
go northward to Milan;
or would he grow
as the others had—son
to the puttana-madonna
in the curse,
chafed by the maternal knot and by
the dream of faithlessness,
uncalloused hands,
lace, white
at the windows of the sailors' brothels
in the port five miles away?
*Soldi*—
*soldi*—
some
worked at the naval yards
and some, like him
were left between
the time the olives turned
from green to black
and the harvest of the grapes,
idle
except for hacking wood.
Those
with an acre of good land
had vines, had wine
and self-respect. Some
carried down crickets

to the garden of the mad Englishwoman
who could
    not
        tolerate
crickets, and they received
    *soldi, soldi*
        for recapturing them . . .
The construction
    continued as heretofore
        on the villa of the Milanese dentist
as the evening
    came in with news:
        —*We have won*
*the election.*
        —*At the café*
            *the red flag is up.*
He turned back
    quickly beneath the tower.
        Giorgino
who wanted to be a waiter
    wanted to be commissar
        piling *sassi*
into the dentist's wall.
    Even the harlot's mother
        who had not dared
come forth because her daughter
    had erred in giving birth,
        appeared by the *Trattoria della Pace.*
She did not enter
    the masculine precinct,
        listening there, her shadow
lengthened-out behind her
    black as the uniform of age
        she wore
on back and head.
    This was the Day
        which began all reckonings
she heard them say
    with a woman's ears;
        she liked
the music from the wireless.
    The padre
        pulled
at his unheeded angelus

and the Day went down behind
the town in the bay below
where—come the season—
they would be preparing
with striped umbrellas,
for the *stranieri* and *milanesi*—
treason so readily compounded
by the promiscuous stir
on the iridescent sliding water.
He had sought
the clear air of the cliff.
*—Salve, Giorgino*
*—Salve*
*Paolo, have you*
heard
*that we have won the election?*
*—I am writing*
*a poem about it:*
*it will begin*
*here, with the cliff and with the sea*
*following its morning shadow in.*


# *Rhenish Winter*

### *a montage after Apollinaire*

In the house
of the vine-grower
women were sewing
*Lenchen*
*pile up the stove*
*put on*
*water for the coffee*
*—Now that the cat*
*has thawed itself*
*it stretches-out flat*
*—Bans are in*
*at last for Gertrude*
*and Martin her neighbour*
The blind nightingale
essayed a song
but quailed in its cage
as the screech-owl wailed

                    *The cypress out there*
*has the air of the pope*
            *setting out in snow*
                        *—That's the post*
*has stopped for a chat*
        *with the new schoolmaster*
                    *—This winter is bitter*
*the wine*
            *will taste all the better*
                *—The sexton*
*the deaf and lame one*
        *is dying*
                *—The daughter*
*of the old burgomaster*
        *is working*
                    *a stole in embroidery*
*for the priest's birthday*
            Out there
                    thanks to the wind
        the forest gave forth
            with its grave organ voice
                    Dreamy Herr Traum
        turned up with his sister
            Frau Sorge
                    unexpectedly
*Mended*
        *you call these*
                *stockings mended Käthe*
*Bring*
        *the coffee the butter the spread*
                *bread in Set*
*the jam and the lard and*
        *don't forget milk*
                *—Lenchen*
*a little more*
        *of that coffee please*
            *—You could imagine*
*that what the wind says*
        *was in Latin*
                *—A little more*
*Lenchen*
        *—Are you sad*
            *Lotte my dear*


                    83

*I think*
        *she's sweet on somebody*
                *—God*
*keep her clear*
        *of that—As for me*
                *I love nobody*
*but myself—Gently*
        *gently*
                *grandmother's telling her rosary*
*—I need*
        *sugar candy*
                *I've a cough Leni*
*—There's Paul*
        *off with his ferret*
                *hunting for rabbits*
The wind
        blew on the firs
                till they danced in a ring
*Love makes*
        *a poor thing of Lotte*
                *Ilse*
*isn't life bright*
        In the snarled stems
                the night
was turning the vineyards
        to charnels of snow
                shrouds
lay there unfolded
        curs
                bayed at cold travellers
*He's dead*
        *listen*
                from the church
the low bell-tone
        The sexton had gone
                *Lise*
*the stove's dwindled to nothing*
        *rekindle it*
                The women
made the sign of the cross
        and the night
                abolished their outline.

84

# The Archer

*for James Dickey*

A lyre at rest:
you fingered it awake
your bow, and showed me
how the tensely-
tempered wood
responded, grew
nimble, lithe
against the bowstring
as you drew. I felt
at once the power
pent in such an instrument
and what your apollonian stance
must now constrain;
then saw the arrows
launch into the lane
of force, and hit
a bale of straw,
impale and pass it
for the earth beyond.
Each time, the string
sang behind their cruel
feathered going
as the sound and scene
combined to one effect—
all rending speed
eyed only
in the aiming, ending.
Mind could not divorce
the wedded terror,
graceful force, and
now must hold their music
single in the silence when
unarrowed, stilled
once more the bow
lay innocent
of what had filled
and bent it to its certainty,
a lyre unstrung,
a kill unsung.

# Winter

It is winter. We have ransacked
 the museums for warmth
  and we have produced garishness.
A Navajo blanket
 woven in a Lancashire factory
  decorates the interior.
It is picturesque
 and we do not want pictures
  but a weather of being
an atmosphere
 that we can inhabit.
  Houses
are built of stone
 pervaded by a locality
  and by durable crafts.
There are no Indians here,
 but it is winter.


# Le Musée Imaginaire

An Aztec sacrifice,
 beside the head of Pope:
  eclectic and unresolvable.
We admire the first
 for its expressiveness, the second
  because we understand it—
can re-create
 its circumstances, and share
  (if not the presuppositions)
the aura
 of the civilities surrounding it.
  The other, in point
at any rate, of violence
 touches us more nearly.
  and yet . . . it is cruel
but unaccountably so; for the temper of awe
 demanded by the occasion, escapes us:
  it is not
better than we are—
 it is merely different.

Expressive, certainly. But of what?
Our loss is absolute, yet unfelt
because inexact. The head
of Alexander Pope,
stiller, attests the more tragic lack
by remaining
what it was meant to be;
intelligible,
it forbids us to approach it.

## At Wells: *polyphony*

The unmoving vault
receives their movement
voices
falling flights
niched
on the sudden, providential hand
of air
daring to reassume
the height that
spanned and hemmed un-
til (like light
entering amber)
they take and hold it
and their time
its space
sustain
in a single element the chord of grace.

## Sea Poem

A whiter bone:
the sea-voice
in a multiple monody
crowding towards that end.
It is as if
the transparencies of sound
composing such whiteness

disposed many layers
        with a sole movement
of the various surface,
        the depths, bottle-glass green
                the bed, swaying
like a fault in the atmosphere, each
        shift
                with its separate whisper, each whisper
a breath of that singleness
        that 'moves together
                if it moves at all',
and its movement is ceaseless,
        and to one end—
                the grinding
a whiter bone.

## The Impalpabilities

It is the sense
        of things that we must include
                because we do not understand them
the impalpabilities
        in the marine dark
                the chords
that will not resolve themselves
        but hang
                in an orchestral undertow
dissolving
        (celeste above shifting strings)
                yet where the dissolution
gathers the echoes
        from an unheard voice:
                and so the wood
advances before the evening takes it—
        branches
                tense in a light like water,
as if (on extended fingers)
        supporting the cool immensity
                while we meditate the strength
in the arms we no longer see.

# *Maillol*

These
    admonitory images
        begotten where
despair alone
    seemed powerful to create
        images commensurate
and durable:
    these
        refusals
of embittered counsels
    of engrossed affections
        celebrate
the earthbound body and
    the full repose,
        or (where
massive Rousillon
    cedes to the glancing grace
        of the Île-de-France)
the delicate
    and perennial recurrences
        of the vineyard and the almond tree.
Paris is sick
    Pomona
        opposes her
carries
    in either extended hand
        the unbitten fruit;
the River
    that still yet flowing
        statue at play
large with its own delight
    and to the shore's
        unfelt restraint
leaning an earthward ear,
    chides the uncivil city
        pours reproof
through its pride of limb.
    These
        caught between sea and mountain
Mediterranean appearances
    were fed

                  by adversity:
no innocence
        unearned
                could glean
what blindness gave
        Aristide Maillol, who
                turned by its threat
from tapestry toward
        an art
                where hand and eye
must marry,
        became
                Maillol the sculptor.
Rather than to express
        his trials or
                his times
in an intricate bravura
        adequate
                to their twists,
he resisted them,
        admired it
                and mistrusted
that flickering frenzy
        of Rodin.
                For poverty had taught
the essential bareness
        bar between
                a plenitude and a luxury.
What tempered
        this disregard for all
                save fecund fact
first principle?—
        Only integrity
                can wear
the bather's bronze
        antique nudity
                and bear
no mirror
        measure
                of the eye's complicity:
here
        hand and eye
                did what conception

bade them do
    enriching it
        with the unforeseen
beauty of the act.
    What fisher
        his customary boat
in measured waters
    can predict
        the catch he fishes?
He knows his net
    but knowledge
        must reassess its ground
to comprehend
    the mystery of fact
        supple in sunlight
teeming from the sound.

# Palm of the Hand

*a version after Rilke*

Palm of the hand. Sole, that no longer walks
except on touch. It is exposed:
a mirror that will give
welcome to heavenly highways
which themselves are fugitive.
Transformer of all turnings,
it has learnt to go
on water, when it scoops it in, to follow
the fountain as it springs.
It enters other hands,
changes its like to landscape,
wanders and returns
in them, its shape
filling them with arrival.

# Flame

Threshing from left to right, whose
    Anger is this? Or whose delight?
For it is volatile like thought, stained-through like mind
    With odour and reminiscence of those seams

Darker and deeper than its shifting scope.
    The mind, that rooted flame
Reaches for knowledge as the flame for hold—
    For shapes and discoveries beyond itself. A slow
Crescendo of crepitations through burning music,
    It mines in its element, shines-out its ores.


## Head Hewn with an Axe

The whittled crystal: fissured
For the invasion of shadows.

The stone book, its
Hacked leaves
Frozen in granite.

The meteorite, anatomized
By the geometer. And to what end?
To the enrichment of the alignment:
Sun against shade against sun:
That daily food, which
Were it not for such importunities
Would go untasted:

The suave block, desecrated
In six strokes. The light
Is staunching its wounds.


## Black Nude

A night-bound fire,
Its cloudy, twisting bulk
Of climbing smoke
Lit by the under-flare:
She stretches, strong
And turning there, recalls it.

All sullen force. What
Can such powers rehearse
Shut in themselves? But see
Her rouse and go
Towards the defining window's
Square of sky.

Less sulkily, the silhouette
Looks out and down
On to the town of roofs
In patterned alternation where
Hard dark is buttressed by hard glare.

Her face receives the sun
And softens it. Angled by
Her arm's embrasure,
White architectured distances
Ride sleeping in the clear truce of her eye.


## Brilliant Silence

Smooth light: all bronze
and polished like a bell
that, biding utterance
hangs heavy with
the fullness that it does not tell.

Yet do not stay too near
the heart of fire, but watch
the way it takes the trees and they
in looming clear, resist it.

Sun-burst: the dam
goes down in silence, feeds
the thirst of shadows, and
brilliance, quiet, distances
attest a counterpointing land.

# Portrait in Stone

*for Henry Gifford*

Face in stone and
Stone in face:
Compacted in this still embrace
Neither displaces either.

The eye that married them,
Grown wiser with the deed,
A twofold matrimony thus
Makes mind and eye unanimous.

The labyrinth of strokes
Has left the rockheart sheer,
That eye and mind may taste the calm
(Want and discord found it there)

And, with their satisfaction, know
The strength that bred this radiance
And brimmed the surface of the stone
To rule a city with a glance.

# The Wrestlers on the Vase

'The flying mare'—that
Throw in wrestling,
Where the winner must
Bring down with grace
And three times
(Stooping, thus)
Take on his shoulder, then
Reverse his man
With, at each throw
An equal craft
Judged and accorded
By the trainer's staff—
That fall's
Applauded here
By circling it
In a second art. A third

Now strives
To gratify (look nimbly!)
Your trainer's eye, and
It will leave
(Should it succeed)
Silence and ease as your sole company.

## Last Judgement

Flame in the pit, flame
In the open height. The same
Unseizable element runs
Bounded and burning
Through that circle of singers
As the damned feel, overflowed
In liquid disorder. Hell
Is the fulfillment which stifles their desire
By granting it.

## The Beech

Nakedly muscular, the beech no longer regrets
Its lost canopy, nor is shamed
By its disorder. The tatters lie
At the great foot. It moves
And what it moves is itself.

## The Tree

I had seen a tree before,
the amputated trunk
merely a table-top
set on a single claw
of roots. But that
was not like this:
this lay awry
even before they cut it;
this—propped up
on the elbows of its boughs

—spanned half a hill
and bridged the green
dank slot
a narrow stream
had worn into the flank
beyond. On end
it leaned against
the rising slope.
Leafless? It was never
leafless. Leaves
climbed with it, roots
socketed and spread into
the layered marl.
And leaves were on it now
that pierced the air
with crumpled wedges—
you could sense the injury
in that half-completed gesture
and before you knew
the cause of it.
This might have seemed
an occasion for regret,
had not the effect
been incontestable.
The saw had entered
sideways the knot of roots,
and the plane it left,
resistant, vertical,
exposed a map
of grains and stains,
a mud-splashed
scored relief
held by a frame,
an inlay lip,
where the rind enclosed it.
The sections of the trunk
greeted each other
from opposing banks
nakedly. A third
irregularly fluted,
now erect,
completed the triangulation,
tugged the group
afresh into a unity

from where it stood
and finally a rain
had cleansed it, freshened,
flushed the colour through.
The reservoir of cóntent,
dammed behind
the mask of form,
the tree's geometry
still put the same
unanswerable question
as the living tree,
though framed it
with a difference, and I
between its Janus faces,
was compelled to echo it,
as though the repetition could
reconsecrate this altar of discarded wood.

# The Gossamers

Autumn. A haze is gold
By definition. This one lit
The thread of gossamers
That webbed across it
Out of shadow and again
Through rocking spaces which the sun
Claimed in the leafage. Now
I saw for what they were
These glitterings in grass, on air,
Of certainties that ride and plot
The currents in their tenuous stride
And, as they flow, must touch
Each blade and, touching, know
Its green resistance. Undefined
The haze of autumn in the mind
Is gold, is glaze.

# The Barometer

It runs ahead. And now
Like all who anticipate
Must wait. Rain was what
Peremptorily it said and
Rain there is none. The air
As still as it, has dimmed
But not with drops, nor with
That sudden progress—when
All that is not black is green—
From intensity to purity. Rain
The repetitive, unmoving finger
Still insists, the name
With numerical corroboration under
Its arrow index. The storm
Hides in the stormhead still
That, heaping-over, spreads
And smokes through the zenith, then
Yields to a sordid-white
Identical image of itself
That climbs, collapsing as before.
The glass door reveals
The figured face, the one
Certainty in all these shifts
Of misty imponderables, pale
Seeping pervasions of each tone,
And the baleful finger
Balances, does not record them.

# Cloud Change

First light—call it
First doubt among shadows
As the seam splits
At sky-level. The dark
Scarcely disperses.
The partial light
Drifts into it from beneath,
Flushes the atmosphere
Transparent. Call it
Dismissal, elemental

Reprimand to reluctance:
The dark is losing
In the day-long sway
That neither can win. Call it—
Defeat into dialogue.


## Letter from Costa Brava

Its crisp sheets, unfolded,
Give on to a grove, where
Citrons conduct the eye
Past the gloom of foliage
Towards the glow of stone. They write
Of a mesmeric clarity
In the fissures of those walls
And of the unseizable lizards, jewelled
Upon them. But let them envy
What they cannot see:
This sodden, variable green
Igniting against the grey.


## Chaconne for Unaccompanied Violin

Here
        walls are cool
                and coolness is
the firm exclusion of a day
                that burns and beats
                        dances at thresholds
and defies
        this moving well
                content
with the ripple-run
        reflected
                in a core of shade.
This
        is the measure
                of a solitude
to feel
        resisting

all that eludes its scope—
to recognize
that music which awaits
the permissive gesture to invade
carrying the single voice against its wave.


## Ship's Waiters

*for Marianne Moore*

Waiters
'gliding'
with the accuracy
and the inscrutable
intuition of the bat,
that avoids collision
even by dark. Nothing
can diminish
that peculiar concert
of either the gliding
man, or the infallible
freaked quadruped, but one
can equal it—
I mean
the leaning fathoms
their pulse
its arterial unpredictable beat
teasing precision from those harried feet.


## The Flight

Foam lips
waters
in following folds
the slow
irrefutable insistence
of the unheard argument
is now behind us
and the immense palm
unrolling its map of wrinkles

bares
    Dakota's rock—
      the Chinese
predicted
  and depicted this
    where cream-white
rises into a wall
  which pinestems (red)
    horizontality of branch
and leaf-mass (rhythmically repeated)
  'decorate' is the word.
    Europe
could not foretell
  that prime vernacular
    made keen
by silence. Lower
  and may the hovering eye
    particularize.

## *Over Brooklyn Bridge*[1]

Mayakovsky
has it!—
    'in the place
of style, an austere
  disposition of bolts.'
    The poet cedes
his elocutionary function[1]
  to the telephone book:
    Helmann
Salinas
  Yarmolinsky,
    words
reciprocally
  kindling one another
    like the train of fire
over a jewel box.
  Miss Moore
    had a negress
for a maid whose father
  was a Cherokee.

[1] 'The poet cedes his elocutionary function . . .' is a slightly travestied version of a famous passage from Mallarmé's *Crise de vers*: 'l'œuvre pure implique la disparation élocutoire du poète, qui cède l'initiative aux mots . . .'

'No', she said
'I do not live in town
            I live in Brooklyn.
            I was afraid
you wouldn't like it here—
            it's gotten so ugly.'
            I liked Brooklyn
with its survival
            of wooden houses
                        and behind trees
the balconies colonnaded.
            And what I liked
                        about the bridge
was the uncertainty
            the way
                        the naked steel
would not go naked
            but must wear
                        its piers of stone—
as the book says
            'stylistically
                        its weakest feature.'
I like
            such weaknesses, the pull
                        the stone base
gives to the armature.
            I live
                        in a place of stone
if it's still there
            by the time I've sailed to it.
                        Goodbye
Miss Moore
            I hope
                        the peacock's feather you once saw
at the house of Ruskin
            has kept its variegations.
                        Jewels
have histories:
            'I never did
                        care for Mallarmé'
she said
            and the words
                        in the book of names
are flames not bolts.

# Ode to Arnold Schoenberg

*on a performance of his concerto for violin*

At its margin
    the river's double willow
        that the wind
variously
    disrupts, effaces
        and then restores
in shivering planes:
    it is
        calm morning.
The twelve notes
    (from the single root
        the double tree)
and their reflection:
    let there be
        unity—this,
however the winds rout
    or the wave disperses
        remains, as
in the liberation of the dissonance
    beauty would seem discredited
        and yet is not:
redefined
    it may be reachieved,
        thus to proceed
through discontinuities
    to the whole in which
        discontinuities are held
like the foam in chalcedony
    the stone, enriched
        by the tones' impurity.
The swayed mirror
    half-dissolves
        and the reflection
yields to reflected light.
    Day. The bell-clang
        goes down the air
and, like a glance
    grasping upon its single thread
        a disparate scene,

crosses and re-creates
        the audible morning.
                All meet at cockcrow
when our common sounds
        confirm our common bonds.
                Meshed in meaning
by what is natural
        we are discontented
                for what is more,
until the thread
        of an instrument pursue
                a more than common meaning.
But to redeem
        both the idiom and the instrument
                was reserved
to this exiled Jew—to bring
        by fiat
                certainty from possibility.
For what is sound
        made reintelligible
                but the unfolded word
branched and budded,
        the wintered tree
                creating, cradling space
and then
        filling it with verdure?

# AMERICAN SCENES
# AND OTHER POEMS
## (1966)

# Face and Image

Between
the image of it
and your face: Between
is the unchartable country,
variable, virgin
terror and territory.

The image—
that most desperate act
of portraiture—
I carry and my mind
marries it willingly,
though the forfeiture's
foreknown already: admit
the reality and you see
the distance from it.

The face—
mouth, eyes and forehead,
substantial things,
advance their frontier
clear against all imaginings:

And yet—
seeing a face, what
do we see?
It is not
the one
incontrovertible you or me.

For, still, we must
in all the trust of seeing
trace
the face in the image, image in the face

To love
is to see,
to let be
this disparateness
and to live within
the unrestricted boundary between.

Even an uncherished face
forces us
to acknowledge
its distinctness, its continuance thus;
then how should these
lips not compound the theme
and being of all appearances?


## The Snow Fences

They are fencing the upland against
the drifts this wind, those clouds
would bury it under: brow and bone
know already that levelling zero
as you go, an aching skeleton,
in the breathtaking rareness of winter air.

Walking here, what do you see?
Little more, through wind-teased eyes,
than a black, iron tree
and, there, another, a straggle
of low and broken wall between, grass
sapped of its greenness, day going.

The farms are few: spread
as wide, perhaps, as when
the Saxons who found them, chose
these airy and woodless spaces
and froze here before they fed
the unsuperseded burial ground.

Ahead, the church's dead-white
limewash will dazzle the mind
as, dazed, you enter to escape:
despite the stillness here, the chill
of wash-light scarcely seems
less penetrant than the hill-top wind.

Between the graves, you find
a beheaded pigeon, the blood and grain
trailed from its bitten crop, as alien to all
the day's pallor as the raw
wounds of the earth, turned above
a fresh solitary burial.

A plaque of staining metal
distinguishes this grave among
an anonymity whose stones
the frosts have scaled, thrusting under
as if they grudged the ground
its ill-kept memorials.

The bitter darkness drives you
back valleywards, and again you bend
joint and tendon to encounter
the wind's force and leave behind
the nameless stones, the snow-shrouds
of a waste season: they are fencing
the upland against those years, those clouds.


# The Fox

When I saw the fox, it was kneeling
in snow: there was nothing to confess
that, tipped on its broken forepaws
the thing was dead—save for its stillness.

A drift, confronting me, leaned down
across the hill-top field. The wind
had scarped it into a pennine wholly of snow, and
where did the hill go now?

There was no way round:
I drew booted legs
back out of it, took to my tracks again,
but already a million blown snow-motes were
flowing and filling them in.

Domed at the summit, then tapering,
the drift still mocked
my mind as if the whole
fox-infested hill were the skull of a fox.

Scallops and dips
of pure pile rippled and shone, but what
should I do with such beauty
eyed by that?

It was like clambering between its white temples
as the crosswind tore
at one's knees, and each
missed step was a plunge at the hill's blinding interior.

## Bone

I unearthed
what seemed like the jawbone of an ass—
and what a weapon it was
that Samson wielded! For the first time
as I drew the soil-stained
haft of it out, I knew.

It balanced
like a hand-scythe, bladed
weighted and curved for an easy blow
that would transmit
the whole of the arm's force as it rose
dropped and dealt it.

How many
was it he slaughtered thus
in a single bout
with just such a boomerang of teeth
grained, greened and barbarous?

But no. Not until I'd cleaned
the weapon did I see
how candidly fleshless
that jawbone must have shone
out of the desert brightness.

A sill now restores it
into perspective, emblem
for a quarrel of deadmen where it lies,
brilliant obstacle beside its shadow
across the pathway of appearances.

# *Wind*

Insistence being of its nature,
thus a refusal to insist is to meet it
on equal terms. For one is neither
bull to bellow with it, nor barometer
to slide, accommodated, into the mood's trough
once the thing has departed. The woods
shook, as though it were the day
of wrath that furrowed its sentence
in the rippled forms, the bleached
obliquity of the winter grass.
Black branches were staggering
and climbing the air, rattling
on one another like a hailfall:
they clawed and tapped, as if the whole
blind company of the dead
bound in its lime, had risen
to repossess this ground. As if—
but time was in mid-career
streaming through space: the dead
were lying in customary quiet.
Kin to the sole bird abroad
gone tinily over like a flung stone,
one hung there against the wind,
blown to a judgment, yes, brought
to bear fronting the airs' commotion.
The noise above, and the rooted silence
under it, poised one in place,
and time said: 'I rescind
the centuries with now,' and space
banishing one from there to here:
'You are not God. You are not the wind.'

# The Door

Too little
has been said
of the door, its one
face turned to the night's
downpour and its other
to the shift and glisten of firelight.

Air, clasped
by this cover
into the room's book,
is filled by the turning
pages of dark and fire
as the wind shoulders the panels, or unsteadies that burning.

Not only
the storm's
breakwater, but the sudden
frontier to our concurrences, appearances,
and as full of the offer of space
as the view through a cromlech is.

For doors
are both frame and monument
to our spent time,
and too little
has been said
of our coming through and leaving by them.


# One World

*One world* you say
eyeing the way the air
inherits it. The year
is dying and the grass
dead that the sunlight burnishes
and breeds distinctions in. Against
its withered grain the shadow
pits and threads it, and your one
lies tracked and tussocked, disparate,
abiding in, yet not obedient

to your whim. Your quiet ministers
to windless air, but the ear
pricks at an under-stir
as the leaves clench tighter
in their shrivellings. The breath of circumstance
is warm, a greeting in their going
and under each death, a birth.


## The Weathercocks

Bitten and burned into mirrors of thin gold,
the weathercocks, blind from the weather,
have their days of seeing as they
grind round on their swivels.

A consciousness of pure metal
begins to melt when (say)
that light 'which never was'
begins to be

And catches the snow's accents
in each dip and lap, and the wide
stains on the thawed ploughland are like continents
across a rumpled map.

Their gold eyes hurt
at the corduroy lines come clear whose grain
feels its way over the shapes of the rises
joining one brown accord of stain and stain.

And the patterning stretches, flown
out on a wing of afternoon cloud that the sun
is changing to sea-wet sandflats,
hummocked in tiny dunes like the snow half-gone—

As if the sole wish of the light
were to harrow with mind matter, to shock
wide the glance of the tree-knots and the stone-eyes
the sun is bathing, to waken the weathercocks.

# *The Hill*

Do not call to her there,
but let her go
bearing our question
in her climb: what does she
confer on the hill, the hill on her?

It shrinks
the personal act and yet
it magnifies
by its barrenly fertile sweep
her very fact.

She
alone, unnamed (as it were),
in making her thought's theme
that thrust and rise,
is bestowing a name:

She inclines
against the current of its resistance,
(as simple as walking, this)
and her bridge-leaner's stance
subdues it with (almost) a willessness.

Nature is hard. Neither the mind
nor the touch can penetrate
to a defenceless part;
but, held on the giant palm, one may negotiate
and she, rising athwart it, is showing the art.

So, do not call to her there:
let her go on,
whom the early sun
is climbing up with to the hill's crown—
she, who did not make it, yet can make
the sun go down by coming down.

# A Given Grace

Two cups,
a given grace,
afloat and white
on the mahogany pool
of table. They unclench
the mind, filling it
with themselves.
Though common ware,
these rare reflections,
coolness of brown
so strengthens and refines
the burning of their white,
you would not wish
them other than they are—
you, who are challenged
and replenished by
those empty vessels.


# Fruit, for Sculpture

A half pear, cool
finial finger
of lute-shaped
abiding fruit.

To eat it?
Who would stir
the white, lit
fallen citadel of its flesh

Without (first)
the thirst of mind and hand
had slaked on
the perfect collusion
of light, knife and tone?

Only
in Eden, does there
ripen a pear of stone.

# Saving the Appearances

The horse is white. Or it
appears to be under this
November light that could
well be October. It goes
as nimbly as a spider does
but it is gainly: the great
field makes it small
so that it seems
to crawl out of the distance
and to grow not larger
but less slow. Stains
on its sides show where
the mud is and the power
now overmasters the fragility
of its earlier bearing. Tall
it shudders over one and bends
a full neck, cropping
the foreground, blotting
the whole space back
behind those pounding feet.
Mounted, one feels the sky
as much the measure of the event
as the field had been, and all
the divisions of the indivisible
unite again, or seem
to do as when the approaching
horse was white, on this
November unsombre day
where what appears, is.

# Through Closed Eyes

Light burns through blood:
a shuttering of shadow brings
the cloud behind the retina, and through
a double darkness, climbs
by the ascent the image is descending
a faceless possible, a form
seeking its sustenance in space.

# In Winter Woods

## 1. *Snow Sequence*

A just-on-the-brink-of-snow feel,
a not-quite-real
access of late daylight. I tread
the puddles' hardness: rents
spread into yard-long splinters—
galactic explosions, outwards
from the stark, amoebic
shapes that air has pocketed
under ice. Even the sky
marbles to accord with grass
and frosted tree: the angles
of the world would be all knives, had not
the mist come up
to turn their edges,
just as the sun began
to slide from this precipice, this pause:
first flakes simultaneously
undid the stillness, scattering
across the disk
that hung, then dropped,
a collapsing bale-fire-red
behind the rimed, now snow-spanned
depth of a disappearing woodland.

## 2. *The Meeting*

Two stand
admiring morning.
A third, unseen as yet
approaches across upland
that a hill and a hill's wood
hide. The two
halving a mutual good,
both watch a sun
entering sideways
the slope of birches
a valley divides them from.
A gauzy steam
smokes from the slope: this
and the light's obliquity

puzzle their glance; they see
thin tree stems:
the knuckled twiggery above
(relieved on sky)
rises more solid
than the thread-fine boles
supporting it—boles that the eye
through its shuttered pane
construes as parallel
scratchings, gold runnels
of paint-drip on the sombre
plane of deeper dark
where the wood evades
the morning. 'But who is this?'
As the third climbs in
down the slope, and the sunlight
clambers with him, on face
and form, 'Who is this?'
they say, who should have asked
'What does he see?' and turned
to answer: a high, bare
unlit hill behind
two faceless visitants
sharing a giant shadow
the night has left: two
at an unseen door
stilled by their question,
whom movement suddenly
humanizes as they
begin descending
through a common day
on to the valley floor.

### 3. *Nocturnal*

Shade confounds shadow now. Blue
is the last tone left
in a wide view
dimming in shrinking vista.
Birds, crossing it,
lose themselves rapidly
behind coverts where all the lines
are tangled, the tangles
hung with a halo of cold dew.

The sun smearily edges
out of the west, and a moon
risen already, will soon
take up to tell in its own style
this tale of confusions:
that light which seemed
to have drawn out after it
all space, melting in horizontals,
must yield now
to a new, tall beam,
a single, judicious eye: it will have
roof behind roof once more, and these
shadows of buildings
must be blocked-in
and ruled with black, and shadows
of black iron must flow
beneath the wrought-iron trees.

### 4. *Focus*

Morning has gone
before the day begins,
leaving an aftermath
of mist, a battleground
burnt-out, still smoking: mist
on the woodslopes like a blue
dank bloom that hazes
a long-browned photograph:
under that monotone
sleep ochres, reds,
and (to the eye
that sees) a burning
of verdure at the vapour's edge
seems to ignite
those half-reluctant tones—
then, having kindled
fails them. Green
in that grey contagion
leads the eye
homewards, to where a black
cut block of fallen beech
turns, in the weathers,
to a muddy anvil:
there, the whole, gigantic

aperture of the day
shuts down to a single
brilliant orifice: a green
glares up through this
out of a dark of whiteness
from the log—a moss
that runs with the grain-mark, whirled
like a river
over a scape of rapids
into a pool of mingling
vortices. And the mind
that swimmer, unabashed
by season, encounters
on entering, places
as intimate as a fire's
interior palaces: an Eden
on whose emerald tinder,
unblinded and unbounded
from the dominance of white,
the heart's eye enkindles.


## The Cavern

Obliterate
mythology as you unwind
this mountain-interior
into the negative-dark mind,
as there
the gypsum's snow
the limestone stair
and boneyard landscape grow
into the identity of flesh.

Pulse of the water-drop,
veils and scales, fins
and flakes of the forming
leprous rock,
how should these
inhuman, turn
human with such chill affinities?

Hard to the hand,
these mosses not of moss,
but nostrils, pits
of eyes, faces
in flight and prints
of feet where no feet ever were,
elude the mind's
hollow that would contain
this canyon within a mountain.

Not far
enough from the familiar,
press
in under a deeper dark until
the curtained sex
the arch, the streaming buttress
have become
the self's unnameable and shaping home.

## *Arizona Desert*

Eye
drinks the dry orange ground,
the cowskull
bound to it by shade:
sun-warped, the layers
of flaked and broken bone
unclench into petals,
into eyelids of limestone:

Blind glitter
that sees
spaces and steppes expand
of the purgatories possible
to us and
impossible.

Upended trees
in the Hopi's desert orchard
betoken
unceasing unspoken war,
return
the levelling light,
imageless arbiter.

A dead snake
pulsates again
as, hidden, the beetles' hunger
mines through the tunnel of its drying skin.

Here, to be,
is to sound
patience deviously
and follow
like the irregular corn
the water underground.

Villages
from mud and stone
parch back
to the dust they humanize
and mean
marriage, a loving lease
on sand, sun, rock and
Hopi
means peace.

## A Death in the Desert

### in memory of Homer Vance

There are no crosses
on the Hopi graves. They lie
shallowly
under a scattering
of small boulders. The sky
over the desert
with its sand-grain stars
and the immense equality

between
desert and desert sky,
seem
a scope and ritual
enough to stem
death and to be its equal.

'Homer
is the name,' said
the old Hopi doll-maker.
I met him in summer. He was dead
when I came back that autumn.

He had sat
like an Olympian
in his cool room
on the rock-roof of the world,
beyond the snatch
of circumstance
and was to die
beating a burro out of his corn-patch.

'That',
said his neighbour
'was a week ago'. And the week
that lay
uncrossably between us
stretched into sand,
into the spread
of the endless
waterless sea-bed beneath
whose space outpacing sight
receded as speechless and as wide as death.


## On the Mountain

Nobody there:
no body,
thin aromatic air
pricking the wide nostrils
that inhale the dark.

Blank brow freezing
where the blaze of snow
carries beyond the summit
up over a satin cloud meadow
to confront the moon.

Nobody sees
the snow-free tree-line,
the aspens weightlessly shivering
and the surrounding pine
that, hardly
lifting their heavy
pagodas of leaves,
yet make a continuous
sound as of sea-wash
around the mountain lake.

And nobody climbs
the dry collapsing ledges
down to the place
to stand
in solitary, sharpened reflection
save for that swaying moon-face.

Somebody
finding nobody there
found gold also:
gold gone, he
(stark in his own redundancy)
must needs go too
and here, sun-warped
and riddled by moon, decays
his house which nobody occupies.


## Las Trampas U.S.A.

*for Robert and Priscilla Bunker*

I go through hollyhocks
in a dry garden, up
to the house,
knock, then ask
in English for the key

to Las Trampas church.
The old woman
says in Spanish: I
do not speak English
so I say: Where
is the church key
in Spanish.
—You see those
three men working: you
ask them. She
goes in, I
go on
preparing to ask
them in Spanish:
Hi, they say
in American. Hello
I say and ask
them in English
where is the key
to the church and they
say: He has it
gesturing to a fourth
man working
hoeing a corn-field
nearby, and to him
(in Spanish): Where is
the church key? And he:
I have it.—O.K.
they say in
Spanish-American:
You bring it (and
to me in English)
He'll bring it. You
wait for him
by the church door.
Thank you, I say and they
reply in American
You're welcome. I go
once more and
await in shadow
the key: he
who brings it is not
he of the hoe, but
one of the three

men working, who
with a Castilian grace
ushers me in
to this place
of coolness out
of the August sun.


## Arroyo Seco

A piano, so long untuned
it sounded like a guitar
was playing *Für Elise*:
the church was locked: graves
on which the only flowers
were the wild ones
except for the everlasting
plastic wreaths and roses,
the bleached dust making
them gaudier than they were
and they were gaudy:

SILVIANO
we loved him
LUCERO

and equal eloquence in
the quotation, twisted and
cut across two pages
in the statuary book:

| THY | LIFE |
|-----|------|
| WILL | BE |
| DO | NE |


## Old Man at Valdez

No books, no songs
belong in the eighty-
year old memory:
he knows where
the Indian graves are

in the woods, recalls
the day the Apaches
crept into Valdez
carrying away
a boy who
forty years later
came back
lacking one arm and said:
'I could hear you all
searching, but I
dursn't cry out
for fear they'd. . .'
The Indians
had trained their prize
to be a one-armed thief.
'And we never did', the old man says,
'see a thief like him
in Valdez.'

*New Mexico*


# Mr. Brodsky

I had heard
before, of an
American who would have preferred
to be an Indian;
but not
until Mr. Brodsky, of one
whose professed and long
pondered-on passion
was to become a Scot,
who even sent for haggis and oatcakes
across continent.
Having read him
in Cambridge English
a verse or two
from MacDiarmid,
I was invited
to repeat the reading
before a Burns Night Gathering
where the Balmoral Pipers
of Albuquerque would

play in the haggis
out of its New York tin.
Of course, I said
No. No. I could *not* go
and then
half-regretted I had not been.
But to console
and cure the wish, came
Mr. Brodsky, bringing
his pipes and played
until the immense, distended
bladder of leather seemed
it could barely contain its water—
tears (idle
tears) for the bridal of Annie Laurie
and Morton J. Brodsky.
A bagpipe in a dwelling is
a resonant instrument
and there he stood
lost in the gorse
the heather or whatever
six thousand
miles and more
from the infection's source,
in our neo-New Mexican parlour
where I had heard
before of an
American who would have preferred
to be merely an Indian.


# Chief Standing Water

### *or my night on the reservation*

Chief Standing Water
explained it

all to me—
the way he

left the reservation
(he was the only

Indian I ever
knew who

favoured explanation
explanation)

then his
conversion

(*Jesus Saves
Courtesy pays*—

the house
was full of texts)

and his
reversion to

'the ways of my people'
though he had

never (as he said)
forfeited

what civilization
taught him—

the house
was full of books

books like *The Book
of Mormon*

a brochure
on the Coronation

a copy of Blavatsky
(left by a former guest)

—her *Secret Doctrine*:
had he

read it? Oh he
had read

it. I like
my reading

heavy
he said:

he played
his drum

to a song
one hundred thousand

years old—
it told

the way his people
had come

from Yucatan
it predicted

the white-man:
you heard

words
like

*Don't know*
*O.K.*

embedded in
the archaic line

quite dis-
tinctly

and listen
he said

there's *Haircut*
and he sang it

again and look
my hair

is cut:
how's that now

for one hundred thousand
years ago

the archaeologists
don't-know-

nothin: and
in farewell:

this is not
he said

a motel but
Mrs. Water and me

we
have our

plans for one
and the next

time that
you come

maybe . . .
I paid

the bill
and considering

the texts
they lived by

he and
Mrs. Water

it was a
trifle high

(*Jesus pays*
*Courtesy saves*)

and that was my
night

on the
reservation.

## At Barstow

Nervy with neons, the main drag
was all there was. A placeless place.
A faint flavour of Mexico in the tacos
tasting of gasoline. Trucks refuelled
before taking off through space. Someone lived
in the houses with their houseyards wired
like tiny Belsens. The Götterdämmerung
would be like this. No funeral pyres, no choirs
of lost trombones. An Untergang
without a clang, without
a glimmer of gone glory
however dimmed. At the motel desk
was a photograph of Roy Rogers
signed. It was here
he made a stay. He did not
ride away on Trigger
through the high night, the tilted
Pleiades overhead, the polestar low, no
going off until
the eyes of beer-cans
had ceased to glint at him
and the desert darknesses
had quenched the neons. He was spent.
He was content. Down he lay.
The passing trucks patrolled his sleep,
the shifted gears contrived
a muffled fugue against the fading of his day
and his dustless, undishonoured stetson rode
beside the bed,
glowed in the pulsating, never-final twilight
there, at that execrable conjunction
of gasoline and desert air.

# Arizona Highway

To become the face of space,
snatching a flowing mask
of emptiness
from where the parallels meet.

One is no more
than invaded transparency, until
on falling asleep, one can feel
them travelling through one still.

The windshield drinks
the telegraphed desert miles,
the tarmac river: tyranny,
glass identity,
devouring and dusty eye,
pure duration, all
transition, transformation.

We have driven into day,
get down to eat:
in a disappearing shadow
under our feet, the dry
pale Sienese reds and oranges
are distinct crystals
that sleep cannot snatch away.

But sleep
expands through senses
that distance has rifled.

When I wake,
hands and head
are in sand, ants are shifting,
inspecting the remains of breakfast,
and on the lips and tongue
burns the fine-ground glass of the sand grains.

# Two Views of Two Ghost Towns

## I

Why speak of memory and death
on ghost ground? Absences
relieve, release. Speak
of the life that uselessness
has unconstrained. Rusting
to its rails, the vast obese
company engine that will draw
no more, will draw no more:
*Keep Off*
the warning says, and all
the mob of objects, freed
under the brightly hard
displacement of the desert light
repeat it: the unaxled wheels,
doorless doors and windowless
regard of space. Clear
of the weight of human
meanings, human need,
gradually
houses splinter to the ground
in white and red, two
rotting parallels beneath
the sombre slag-mound.

## II

How dry the ghosts
of dryness are. The air
here, tastes of sparseness
and the graveyard stones
are undecorated. To the left
the sea and, right, the shadows
hump and slide, climbing
the mountainside as clouds go over.
The town has moved away,
leaving a bitten hill
where the minehead's visible. Brambles
detain the foot. Ketchum,
Clay, Shoemake, Jebez O'Haskill
and Judge H. Vennigerholz
all (save for the judge's

modest obelisk) marked
by a metal cross; and there are four
crosses of wood, three
wooden stakes (unnamed)
that the sun, the frost, the sea-
wind shred alternately
in sapless scars. How dry
the ghosts of dryness are.


## Ute Mountain

'When I am gone'
the old chief said
'if you need me, call me',
and down he lay, became stone.

They were giants then
(as you may see),
and we
are not the shadows of such men.

The long splayed Indian hair
spread ravelling out
behind the rocky head
in groins, ravines;

petered across the desert plain
through Colorado,
transmitting force
in a single undulant unbroken line

from toe to hair-tip: there
profiled, inclined away from one
are features, foreshortened, and the high
blade of the cheekbone.

Reading it so, the eye
can take the entire great
straddle of mountain-mass,
passing down elbows, knees and feet.

'If you need me, call me.'
His singularity dominates the plain
as we call to our aid his image:
thus men make a mountain.


## In Connecticut

White, these villages. White
their churches without altars. The first snow
falls through a grey-white sky
and birch-twig whiteness turns
whiter against the grey. White
the row of pillars (each
of them is a single tree), the walls
sculptureless. 'This church was gathered
in 1741. In 1742
by act of the General Assembly of Connecticut
this territory was incorporated
and was named Judea.'
The sun passes, the elms
enter as lace shadows, then
go out again. White . . .
'Our minister is fine. He's a minister
in church, and a man outside.'—delivered
with the same shadowless conviction
as her invitation, when
lowering, leaning
out of the window she was cleaning
she had said: 'Our doors
are always open.'


## Maine Winter

Ravenous the flock
who with an artist's
tact, dispose
their crow-blue-black
over the spread of snow—

Trackless, save where
by stalled degrees
a fox flaringly goes
with more of the hunter's caution than
of the hunter's ease.

The flock
have sighted him, are his match
and more, with their artist's eye
and a score of beaks against
a fox, paws clogged, and a single pair of jaws.

And they mass to the red-on-white
conclusion, sweep
down between
a foreground all snow-scene and a distance
all cliff-tearing seascape.


# Letters from Amherst

### for Edith Perry Stamm

Letters from Amherst came. They were written
In so peculiar a hand, it seemed
The writer might have learned the script by studying
The famous fossil bird-tracks
In the museum of that college town. Of punctuation
There was little, except for dashes: 'My companion
Is a dog', they said, 'They are better
Than beings, because they know but do not tell.'
And in the same, bird-like script: 'You think
My gait "spasmodic". I am in danger, sir.
You think me uncontrolled. I have no tribunal.'
Of people: 'They talk of hallowed things aloud
And embarrass my dog. I let them hear
A noiseless noise in the orchard. I work
In my prison where I make
Guests for myself.' The first of these
Letters was unsigned, but sheltered
Within the larger package was a second,
A smaller, containing what the letter lacked—
A signature, written upon a card in pencil,

As if the writer wished
To recede from view as far as possible
In the upstairs room
In the square cool mansion where she wrote
Letters from Amherst . . .

## *In Longfellow's Library*

Sappho
and the Venus de Milo
gaze out past
the scintillations from
the central
candelabrum
to where
(on an upper shelf)
plaster Goethe
in a laurel
crown, looks
down divided
from a group
dancing a
tarantella, by
the turquoise butterfly
that Agassiz
brought back
dead: below
these, the busts of
Homer, Aeschylus
and Sophocles still
pedestalled where
they ambushed Hiawatha.

## *On Eleventh Street*

A mosaicist of minute
attentions composed it,
arranged the gravel
walks, where there is not
room for any, and the neat

hedges of privet: the complete
Second Cemetery
of the Spanish and Portuguese
Synagogue, Shearith
Israel, in the City of
New York
eighteen-five to
twenty-nine, could be
cut out, and carried
away by three
men, one at each
corner: a tight
triangle between two
building ends, the third
side a wall, white-washed
topped by a railing, and a gate
in it on to the street.


# A Garland for Thomas Eakins

### for Seymour Adelman

## I

He lived
from his second year
at seventeen twentynine
Mount Vernon Street
Philadelphia
Pennsylvania where
he painted his
father and his sisters
and he died
in Pennsylvania in
Philadelphia at
seventeen twentynine
Mount Vernon Street.

## II

Anatomy, perspective
and reflection: a boat
in three inclinations:
to the wind, to the waves
and to the picture-frame.
Those are the problems. What
does a body propose
that a boat does not?

## III

Posing the model
for 'The Concert Singer' he
stood her
relative to a grid
placed vertically
behind her. There was a spot
before her
on the wall that
she must look at.
To her dress
by the intersections
of the grid he tied
coloured ribbons, thus
projecting her
like an architect's elevation
on a plane
that was vertical, the canvas
at a right angle
to the eye and perpendicular
to the floor.
What does the man
who sees
trust to
if not the eye? He trusts
to knowledge
to right appearances.

## IV

—And what do you think of
that, Mr. Eakins? (A Whistler)
—I think that that
is a very cowardly way to paint.

A fat woman
by Rubens
is not a fat
woman but a fiction.

VI

The Eakins portrait
(said Whitman)
sets me down
in correct style
without feathers.
And when they
said to him:
Has Mr. Eakins no
social gifts? he said
to them: What are
'social gifts'?—
The parlour puts
quite its own
measure upon social gifts.

VII

The figures of perception
as against
the figures of elocution.
What they wanted
was to be Medici
in Philadelphia
and they survive
as Philadelphians.

VIII

The accord with that
which asked
only to be recorded:
'How beautiful,' he said,
'an old lady's skin is:
all those wrinkles!'

IX

*Only*
to be recorded!
and his stare
in the self-portrait
calculates the abyss
in the proposition. He dies
unsatisfied, born
to the stubborn
anguish of
those eyes.

## The Well

*in a Mexican convent*

Leaning on
the parapet stone
Listening down
the long, dark
sheath through which the standing
shaft of water
sends its echoings up
Catching, as it stirs
the steady seethings
that mount and mingle
with surrounding sounds
from the neighbouring
barrack-yard: soldiery
—heirs, no doubt
of the gunnery that gashed
these walls of tattered
frescoes, the bullet-
holes now socketed
deeper by sunlight
and the bright gaps
giving on to the square
and there revealing
strollers in khaki
with their girls Aware
of a well-like
cool throughout
the entire, clear
sunlit ruin,

142

of the brilliant cupids
above the cistern
that hold up
a baldachin of stone
which is not there
Hearing the tide
of insurrection
subside through time
under the still-
painted slogans
*Hemos servido*
*lealmente*
*la revolución*

## On a Mexican Straw Christ

This is not the event. This
Is a man of straw,
The legs straw-thin
The straw-arms shent
And nailed. And yet this dry
Essence of agony must be
Close-grained to the one
They lifted down, when
*Consummatum est* the event was done.
Below the baroque straw-
Haloed basket-head
And the crown, far more
Like a cap, woven
For a matador than a crown of thorn,
A gap recedes: it makes
A mouth-in-pain, the teeth
Within its sideways-slashed
And gritted grin, are
Verticals of straw, and they
Emerge where the mask's
Chin ceases and become
Parallels plunging down, their sum
The body of God. Beneath,
Two feet join in one
Cramped culmination, as if
To say: 'I am the un-
Resurrection and the Death.'

# On the Tlacolula Bus

On the Tlacolula bus
'I flew for the Fuehrer'
it says: *Yo volé*
*para el Fuehrer* signed
*Lukenbac* in Gothic.
The Fuehrer is dead and Lukenbac
does not drive today:
instead, a Mexican with the brown
face of a Mayan
is in his place and under
a sign *No distraer*
*al Operador* is
chatting across his shoulder.
Would Lukenbac? And does he
care for this country, or long
for a land of hygiene and Christmas trees
where he would not dare
write up his boast in Gothic?
As we swing
out of the market square
a goat on a string
being led by someone
stops, stands and while
the bus passes by
into history, turns
on the succession of windows
its narrow stare, looking
like Lukenbac in exile.


# The Oaxaca Bus

*Fiat Voluntas Tua:*
over the head of the driver
an altar. No end to it,
the beginning seems to be
Our Lady of Solitude
blessing the crowd
out of a double frame—
gilt and green. Dark
mother by light,

her neighbour, the Guadalupe Virgin
is tucked away under the right-
hand edge as if
to make sure
twice over and (left)
are the legs of a protruding
post-card crucifixion
mothered by both. A cosmos
proliferates outwards
from the mystery, starts
with the minute, twin
sombreros dangling there, each
with embroidered brims
and a blood-red cord
circling the crown of each.
The driving mirror
catches their reflection, carries on
the miraculous composition
with two names—serifs
and flourishes—: *Maria,*
*Eugenia*: both
inscribed on the glass and
flanked at either end
by rampant rockets
torpedoing moonwards. Again
on either side,
an artificial vine
twines down: it is tied
to rails in the aisle
and, along it, flower—
are they nasturtiums? They are
pink like the bathing dresses
of the cut-out belles
it passes in descending,
their petals are pleated
like the green
of the fringed curtain that borders the windshield:
they are lilies
of the field of Mexico,
plastic godsend,
last flourish
of that first *Fiat* from sister goddesses
and (yes)
the end . . .

# Constitution Day

Subject for Eisenstein
but in reversion:
proletariat
flowing in cinematic streams
all going the wrong way
to pray
to the Dark Virgin of Tepeyac hill.

Ablaze
in his laundered white
an adolescent recites
a poem on the Constitution
and, *Juarez, Madero, Cárdenas*
the names go by
like faces in a fresco
just as Diego
would have painted them. It's all
very bad, but it's a poem.

While the brass band
finger their instruments for another fanfare
—*Juarez, Lopez Mateos*—
penitents come pouring in
to the gold interior and effigy,
deaf to the Day and seeking
the promise of a more than human mercy.

The committee
platformed behind the spouting child
are quite the best-
dressed Mexicans I have seen,
perched there beyond the doom
of the ragged rest,
of God's desolate mother, Eisenstein
dead of a weakened heart
and Stalin rifled from his tomb.

# The Bootblack

What does he think about
down there? His hair is immaculate
and all that I can glimpse
save for a pair of hands
in a mess of turpentine, the back
thin, its twin shoulder-blades
rucking the shirt. What does he see?
Does he see me? Or the penitents
behind him, crossing the plaza
by the Basilica de Guadalupe
and climbing
up into the shrine
taking the steps on shuffled knees?
It's Constitution Day.
Does he care? Does he hear
the processions of bobbing straw sombreros
on sandalled feet
liquid-footed as sheep
feeding the city from the villages?
Ask your questions, and they
reply with smiles you cannot interpret.
He has done
spreading the stain
from naked fingers, has put on
the shine. I say: 'The shoes
are fit for a king.' And he smiles.
Will he be
angry or mirthful when he
inherits the earth?

*Mexico City*

# Theory of Regress

Seven bulls of a Sunday:
corrida for the crowd, carcasses
for the penitentiary. *And you descend*
said Artaud, *to this*
*when you began*
*with human*
*sacrifice?*

147

# In Michoacán

A poor church
but an obstinate devotion
had filled it
with flowers.

What power drew
those flower-fraught Indians down
by narrow trails
no one knew

Until the earthquake:
after it, the altar
split wide open
like a hell-mouth,

And inside the wreck
there sat
its guardian idol:
squat, smiling, Aztec.

# Weeper in Jalisco

A circle of saints, all
hacked, mauled, bound,
bleed in a wooden frieze
under the gloom of the central
dome of gold. They
are in paradise now
and we are not—
baroque feet gone
funnelling up, a blood-
bought, early resurrection
leaving us this
tableau of wounds, the crack
in the universe sealed
behind their flying backs.
We are here, and a woman
sprawls and wails to them
there, the gold screen
glistening, hemming her

under, till her keening
fills the stone ear
of the whole, hollow sanctum
and she is the voice
those wounds cry through
unappeasably bleeding where
her prone back shoulders
the price and weight
of forfeited paradise.


# Landscape

### after Octavio Paz

Rock and precipice,
More time than stone, this
Timeless matter.

Through its cicatrices
Falls without moving
Perpetual virgin water.

Immensity reposes here
Rock over rock,
Rocks over air.

The world's manifest
As it is: a sun
Immobile, in the abyss.

Scale of vertigo:
The crags weigh
No more than our shadows.


# Idyll

### Washington Square, San Francisco

A door:
      *PER L'UNIVERSO*
            is what it says
above it.

You must approach
more nearly
(the statue
of Benjamin Franklin watching you)
before you see
*La Gloria di Colui*
*che tutto muove*
***PER L'UNIVERSO***
—leaning
along the lintel—
*penetra e risplende*
across this church
for Italian Catholics:
Dante
unscrolling in rhapsody.
Cool
the January sun.
that with an intensity
the presence of the sea
makes more exact,
chisels the verse with shade
and lays
on the grass
a deep and even
Californian green,
while a brilliance
throughout the square
flatters the meanness of its architecture.
Beyond
there is the flood
which skirts this pond
and tugs the ear
towards it: cars
thick on the gradients of the city
shift sun and sound—
a constant ground-bass
to these provincialisms of the piazza
tasting still
of Lerici and Genova.
Here
as there
the old men sit
in a mingled odour
of cheroot and garlic

spitting;
		they share serenity
				with the cross-legged
Chinese adolescent
		seated between them
				reading, and whose look
wears the tranquility of consciousness
		forgotten in its object—
				his book
bears for a title
		*SUCCESS*
				*in spelling.*
How
		does one spell out this
				*che penetra e risplende*
from square
		into the hill-side alley-ways
				around it, where
between tall houses
		children of the Mediterranean
				and Chinese element
mingle
		their American voices? . . .
				The dictionary
defines idyllium
		as meaning
				'a piece, descriptive
chiefly of rustic life';
		we
				are in town: here
let it signify
		this poised quiescence, pause
				and possibility in which
the music of the generations
		binds into its skein
				the flowing instant,
while the winter sun
		pursues the shadow
				before a church
whose decoration
		is a quotation from *Paradiso.*

# Small Action Poem

*for Robert and Bobbie Creeley*

To arrive
      unexpectedly
            from nowhere:
then:
      having done
            what it was
one came for,
      to depart.
            The door
is open now
      that before
            was neither
open
      nor was it there.
            It is like
Chopin
      shaking
            music from the fingers,
making that
      in which
            all is either
technique
      heightened to sorcery
            or nothing but notes.
To arrive
      unexpectedly
            at somewhere
and the final
      chord, the final
            word.

# THE WAY OF A WORLD
## (1969)

*Y tanto se da el presente*
*Que el pie caminante siente*
*La integridad del planeta.*
Jorge Guillén, *Perfección*

# Swimming Chenango Lake

Winter will bar the swimmer soon.
  He reads the water's autumnal hesitations
A wealth of ways: it is jarred,
  It is astir already despite its steadiness,
Where the first leaves at the first
  Tremor of the morning air have dropped
Anticipating him, launching their imprints
  Outwards in eccentric, overlapping circles.
There is a geometry of water, for this
  Squares off the clouds' redundances
And sets them floating in a nether atmosphere
  All angles and elongations: every tree
Appears a cypress as it stretches there
  And every bush that shows the season,
A shaft of fire. It is a geometry and not
  A fantasia of distorting forms, but each
Liquid variation answerable to the theme
  It makes away from, plays before:
It is a consistency, the grain of the pulsating flow.
  But he has looked long enough, and now
Body must recall the eye to its dependence
  As he scissors the waterscape apart
And sways it to tatters. Its coldness
  Holding him to itself, he grants the grasp,
For to swim is also to take hold
  On water's meaning, to move in its embrace
And to be, between grasp and grasping, free.
  He reaches in-and-through to that space
The body is heir to, making a where
  In water, a possession to be relinquished
Willingly at each stroke. The image he has torn
  Flows-to behind him, healing itself,
Lifting and lengthening, splayed like the feathers
  Down an immense wing whose darkening spread
Shadows his solitariness: alone, he is unnamed
  By this baptism, where only Chenango bears a name
In a lost language he begins to construe—
  A speech of densities and derisions, of half-
Replies to the questions his body must frame
  Frogwise across the all but penetrable element.
Human, he fronts it and, human, he draws back
  From the interior cold, the mercilessness

That yet shows a kind of mercy sustaining him.
   The last sun of the year is drying his skin
Above a surface a mere mosaic of tiny shatterings,
   Where a wind is unscaping all images in the flowing obsidian,
The going-elsewhere of ripples incessantly shaping.


## *Prometheus*[1]

Summer thunder darkens, and its climbing
   Cumulae, disowning our scale in the zenith,
Electrify this music: the evening is falling apart.
   Castles-in-air; on earth: green, livid fire.
The radio simmers with static to the strains
   Of this mock last-day of nature and of art.

We have lived through apocalypse too long:
   Scriabin's dinosaurs! Trombones for the transformation
That arrived by train at the Finland Station,
   To bury its hatchet after thirty years in the brain
Of Trotsky. Alexander Nikolayevitch, the events
   Were less merciful than your mob of instruments.

Too many drowning voices cram this waveband.
   I set Lenin's face by yours—
Yours, the fanatic ego of eccentricity against
   The systematic son of a schools inspector
Tyutchev on desk—for the strong man reads
   Poets as the antisemite pleads: 'A Jew was my friend.'

Cymballed firesweeps. Prometheus came down
   In more than orchestral flame and Kérensky fled
Before it. The babel of continents gnaws now
   And tears at the silk of those harmonies that seemed
So dangerous once. You dreamed an end
   Where the rose of the world would go out like a close in music.

Population drags the partitions down
   And we are a single town of warring suburbs:
I cannot hear such music for its consequence:
   Each sense was to have been reborn

[1] 'Prometheus' refers to the tone-poem by Scriabin and to his hope of transforming the world by music and rite.

Out of a storm of perfumes and light
  To a white world, an in-the-beginning.

In the beginning, the strong man reigns:
  Trotsky, was it not then you brought yourself
To judgement and to execution, when you forgot
  Where terror rules, justice turns arbitrary?
Chromatic Prometheus, myth of fire,
  It is history topples you in the zenith.

Blok, too, wrote The Scythians
  Who should have known: he who howls
With the whirlwind, with the whirlwind goes down.
  In this, was Lenin guiltier than you
When, out of a merciless patience grew
  The daily prose such poetry prepares for?

Scriabin, Blok, men of extremes,
  History treads out the music of your dreams
Through blood, and cannot close like this
  In the perfection of anabasis. It stops. The trees
Continue raining though the rain has ceased
  In a cooled world of incessant codas:

Hard edges of the houses press
  On the after-music senses, and refuse to burn,
Where an ice cream van circulates the estate
  Playing Greensleeves, and at the city's
Stale new frontier even ugliness
  Rules with the cruel mercy of solidities.


# A Dream

### or the worst of both worlds

Yevtushenko, Voznesensky and I
are playing to a full house: I lack their verve
(I know) their red reserve
of Scythian corpuscles, to ride in triumph through
Indianapolis. They read. Libido roars
across the dionysian sluice of the applause
and the very caryatids lean down
to greet them: youth towers (feet

on shoulders) into instant acrobatic pyramids—
human triforia to shore up the roof
cheering. I come on
sorting my pages, searching for the one
I've failed to write. It's October
nineteen seventeen once more. But is it me
or Danton from the tumbril, stentoriously
starts delivering one by one my bits of ivory?
No matter. I still ride their tide of cheers
and I could read the whole sheaf
backwards, breasting effortlessly
the surge of sweat and plaudits to emerge
laurelled in vatic lather, brother, bard:
the hear me out who have not heard one word,
bringing us back for bows, bringing down the house
once more. The reds return to their homeground stadia,
their unforeseen disgraces; I
to the sobriety of a dawn-cold bed, to own
my pariah's privilege, my three-inch spaces,
the reader's rest and editor's colophon.

## A Word in Edgeways

Tell me about yourself they
say and you begin to
tell them about yourself and
that is just the way I
am is their reply: they play
it all back to you in another
key, their key, and then in mid-
narrative they pay you a
compliment as if to say what a good
listener you are I am
a good listener my stay
here has developed my faculty I will
say that for me I will not
say that every literate male in
America is a soliloquist, a
ventriloquist, a strategic
egotist, an inveterate
campaigner-explainer over and
back again on the terrain of him-

self—what I will
say is they are not un-
interesting: they are simply
unreciprocal and yes it was a
pleasure if not an unmitigated
pleasure and I yes I did enjoy our
conversation goodnightthankyou

## *Eden*

I have seen Eden. It is a light of place
   As much as the place itself; not a face
Only, but the expression on that face: the gift
   Of forms constellates cliff and stones:
The wind is hurrying the clouds past,
   And the clouds as they flee, ravelling-out
Shadow a salute where the thorn's barb
   Catches the tossed, unroving sack
That echoes their flight. And the same
   Wind stirs in the thicket of the lines
In Eden's wood, the radial avenues
   Of light there, copious enough
To draft a city from. Eden
   Is given one, and the clairvoyant gift
Withdrawn, 'Tell us,' we say
   'The way to Eden', but lost in the meagre
Streets of our dispossession, where
   Shall we turn, when shall we put down
This insurrection of sorry roofs? Despair
   Of Eden is given, too: we earn
Neither its loss nor having. There is no
   Bridge but the thread of patience, no way
But the will to wish back Eden, this leaning
   To stand against the persuasions of a wind
That rings with its meaninglessness where it sang its meaning.

# Adam

Adam, on such a morning, named the beasts:
   It was before the sin. It is again.
An openwork world of lights and ledges
   Stretches to the eyes' lip its cup:
Flower-maned beasts, beasts of the cloud,
   Beasts of the unseen, green beasts
Crowd forward to be named. Beasts of the qualities
   Claim them: sinuous, pungent, swift:
We tell them over, surround them
   In a world of sounds, and they are heard
Not drowned in them; we lay a hand
   Along the snakeshead, take up
The nameless muzzle, to assign its vocable
   And meaning. Are we the lords or limits
Of this teeming horde? We bring
   To a kind of birth all we can name
And, named, it echoes in us our being.
   Adam, on such a morning, knew
The perpetuity of Eden, drew from the words
   Of that long naming, his sense of its continuance
And of its source—beyond the curse of the bitten apple—
   Murmuring in wordless words: 'When you deny
The virtue of this place, then you
   Will blame the wind or the wide air,
Whatever cannot be mastered with a name,
   Mouther and unmaker, madman, Adam.'

# Night Transfigured

Do you recall the night we flung
   Our torch-beam down in among
The nettle towers? Stark-white
   Robbed of their true dimension
Or of the one we knew, their dense
   World seemed to be all there was:
An immense, shifting crystal
   Latticed by shadow, it swayed from the dark,
Each leaf, lodged blade above blade
   In serrated, dazzling divisions.

What large thing was it stood
   In such small occurence, that it could
Transfigure the night, as we
   Drew back to find ourselves once more
In the surrounding citadel of height and air?
   To see then speak, is to see with the words
We did not make. That silence
   Loud with the syllables of the generations, and that sphere
Centred by a millenial eye, all that was not
   There, told us what was, and clothed
The sense, bare as it seemed, in the weave
   Of years: we knew that we were sharers,
Heirs to the commonalty of sight, that the night
   In its reaches and its nearnesses, possessed
A single face, sheer and familiar
   Dear if dread. The dead had distanced,
Patterned its lineaments, and to them
   The living night was cenotaph and ceaseless requiem.


# *Assassin*

*The rattle in Trotsky's throat and his wild boar's moans*
                        *Piedra de Sol* (Octavio Paz)

Blood I foresaw. I had put by
   The distractions of the retina, the eye
That like a child must be fed and comforted
   With patterns, recognitions. The room
Had shrunk to a paperweight of glass and he
   To the centre and prisoner of its transparency.

He rasped pages. I knew too well
   The details of that head. I wiped
Clean the glance and saw
   Only his vulnerableness. Under my quivering
There was an ease, save for that starched insistence
   While paper snapped and crackled as in October air.

Sound drove out sight. We inhabited together
    One placeless cell. I must put down
This rage of the ear for discrimination, its absurd
    Dwelling on ripples, liquidities, fact
Fastening on the nerve gigantic paper burs.
    The gate of history is straiter than eye's or ear's.

In imagination, I had driven the spike
    Down and through. The skull had sagged in its blood.
The grip, the glance—stained but firm—
    Held all at its proper distance and now hold
This autumnal hallucination of white leaves
    From burying purpose in a storm of sibilance.

I strike. I am the future and my blow
    Will have it now. If lightning froze
It would hover as here, the room
    Riding in the crest of the moment's wave,
In the deed's time, the deed's transfiguration
    And as if that wave would never again recede.

The blood wells. Prepared for this
    This I can bear. But papers
Snow to the ground with a whispered roar:
    The voice, cleaving their crescendo, is his
Voice, and his the animal cry
    That has me then by the roots of the hair.

Fleshed in that sound, objects betray me,
    Objects are my judge: the table and its shadow,
Desk and chair, the ground a pressure
    Telling me where it is that I stand
Before wall and window-light:
    Mesh of the curtain, wood, metal, flesh:

A dying body that refuses death,
    He lurches against me in his warmth and weight,
As if my arm's length blow
    Had transmitted and spent its strength
Through blood and bone; and I, spectred,
    The body that rose against me were my own.

Woven from the hair of that bent head,
   The thread that I had grasped unlabyrinthed all—
Tightrope of history and necessity—
   But the weight of a world unsteadies my feet
And I fall into the lime and contaminations
   Of contingency; into hands, looks, time.


## Against Extremity

Let there be treaties, bridges,
   Chords under the hands, to be spanned
Sustained: extremity hates a given good
   Or a good gained. That girl who took
Her life almost, then wrote a book
   To exorcise and to exhibit the sin,
Praises a friend there for the end she made
   And each of them becomes a heroine.
The time is in love with endings. The time's
   Spoiled children threaten what they will do,
And those they cannot shake by petulance
   They'll bribe out of their wits by show.
Against extremity, let there be
   Such treaties as only time itself
Can ratify, a bond and test
   Of sequential days, and like the full
Moon slowly given to the night,
   A possession that is not to be possessed.


## In the Fullness of Time

### a letter to Octavio Paz

The time you tell us is the century and the day
   Of Shiva and Parvati: imminent innocence,
Moment without movement. Tell us, too, the way
   Time, in its fullness, fills us
As it flows: tell us the beauty of succession
   That Breton denied: the day goes
Down, but there is time before it goes
   To negotiate a truce in time. We met
Sweating in Rome and in a place
   Of confusions, cases and telephones: and then

163

It was evening over Umbria, the train
   Arriving, the light leaving the dry fields
And next the approaching roofs. As we slowed
   Curving towards the station, the windows ahead swung
Back into our line of vision and flung at us
   A flash of pausing lights: the future
That had invited, waited for us there
   Where the first carriages were. That hesitant arc
We must complete by our consent to time—
   Segment to circle, chance into event:
And how should we not consent? For time
   Putting its terrors by, it was as if
The unhurried sunset were itself a courtesy.


## Music's Trinity

*Lugar de las nupcias impalpables*
(for Octavio and Marie José)


Motion: not things
moving, where the harp's
high swan
sailing out across
clear water
has all our ear.

Time: not the crabbed
clock's, but the force
and aggregation as the horns'
cumulae mass
rising to rob the sky
of silence.

Space: not between
but where: as,
out of a liquid
turbulence, a tremulousness gives place
to Atlantis.

# Logic

A trailed and lagging grass, a pin-point island
Drags the clear current's face it leans across
In ripple-wrinkles. At a touch
It has ravelled the imaged sky till it could be
A perplexity of metal, spun
Round a vortex, the sun flung off it
Veining the eye like a migraine—it could
Scarcely be sky. The stones do more, until we say
We see there meshes of water, liquid
Nets handed down over them, a clear
Cross-hatching in the dance of wrinkles that
Re-patterns wherever it strikes.
So much for stones. They seem to have their way.
But the sway is the water's: it cannot be held
Though moulded and humped by the surfaces
It races over, though a depth can still
And a blade's touch render it illegible.
Its strength is here: it must
Account for its opposite and yet remain
Itself, of its own power get there.
Water is like logic, for it flows
Meeting resistance arguing as it goes:
And it arrives, having found not the quickest
Way, but the way round, the channel which
Entering, it may come to a level in,
Which must admit, in certain and crowding fusion,
The irrefutable strength which follows it.


# The Way of a World

Having mislaid it, and then
    Found again in a changed mind
The image of a gull the autumn gust
    Had pulled upwards and past
The window I watched from, I recovered too
    The ash-key, borne-by whirling
On the same surge of air, like an animate thing:
    The scene was there again: the bird,
The seed, the windlines drawn in the sidelong
    Sweep of leaves and branches that only

165

The black and supple boughs restrained—
  All would have joined in the weightless anarchy
Of air, but for that counterpoise. All rose
  Clear in the memory now, though memory did not choose
Or value it first: it came
  With its worth and, like those tree-tips,
Fine as dishevelling hair, but steadied
  And masted as they are, that worth
Outlasted its lost time, when
  The cross-currents had carried it under.
In all these evanescences of daily air,
  It is the shapes of change, and not the bare
Glancing vibrations, that vein and branch
  Through the moving textures: we grasp
The way of a world in the seed, the gull
  Swayed toiling against the two
Gravities that root and uproot the trees.


## Descartes and the Stove

Thrusting its armoury of hot delight,
  Its negroid belly at him, how the whole
Contraption threatened to melt him
  Into recognition. Outside, the snow
Starkened all that snow was not—
  The boughs' nerve-net, angles and gables
Denting the brilliant hoods of it. The foot-print
  He had left on entering, had turned
To a firm dull gloss, and the chill
  Lined it with a fur of frost. Now
The last blaze of day was changing
  All white to yellow, filling
With bluish shade the slots and spoors
  Where, once again, badger and fox would wind
Through the phosphorescence. All leaned
  Into that frigid burning, corded tight
By the lightlines as the slow sun drew
  Away and down. The shadow, now,
Defined no longer: it filled, then overflowed
  Each fault in snow, dragged everything
Into its own anonymity of blue
  Becoming black. The great mind

Sat with his back to the unreasoning wind
  And doubted, doubted at his ear
The patter of ash and, beyond, the snow-bound farms,
  Flora of flame and iron contingency
And the moist reciprocation of his palms.


# The Question

Having misread the house, 'What
  Room is it,' she said, 'lies beyond
That?' And towards the door
  Which did not exist, leaned
The room of air, the thousand directions
  Ungoverned by any eye save one—
The blind house-wall, that for its two
  Centuries had faced away
From that long possession of the moon and sun,
  Room of the damasked changes where
Tonight, a pentecostal storm-light
  Flashed and died through its patternings
And each invisible scene replied
  In echo, tree-lash and water-voice
With the gift of tongues. In the room of storm
  Rain raked the confine with its dense
Volley, the old house staining
  Through wall and floor, as the sodden
Clamorous earth exuded, locked
  Round on its soundlessness, but turned
Towards her question: 'What
  Room is it lies beyond that?'


# The View

The woods are preparing to wait out winter.
  Gusts blow with an earnest of all there is to be done
Once frost will have entered the apple and the sun.
  Of the view, there is no tale to tell you.
Its history is incidental. One would not date
  The window that stands open like a gate
In the opposing house-face. It is dark inside.
  The façade is a dirty white, and yet it seems

The right colour to stand there between
   The dull green of the foreground trees
Still bearing leaves, and the autumnal glare
   From the others framing it, foregoing theirs.
The dark of the window square might be
   A mineshaft of pure shadow, a way
Through to the heart of the hill—the black
   Centre, if centre there were where
Sight must travel such drops and intervals,
   And an undulation of aspens along the slope
Is turning the wind to water and to light,
   Unpivoting place amid its shaken coins,
While under a shuddering causeway, a currency,
   The season is dragging at all the roots of the view.


# *Weatherman*

Weather releases him from the tyranny of rooms,
   From the white finality of clapboard towns.
The migrations have begun: geese going
   Wake him towards dawn, as they stream south
Drawing the north behind them, the long threat
   That disquiets his blood. He rises and roams
In the grey house. In the dark
   Height, geese yelp like a pack
Hunting through space. Unseen, they drive the eye
   Of the mind the way they go, through the opal
Changes of dawn light on the light of snow.
   The sun looks full at the town, at each
House with its double fringe of icicles
   And their shadows. He can hear no more
The cries that had woken him, but through eyes
   That wincing away from it, blink back
The radiance that followed the flock, he drinks in
   Human his inheritance and retrieved his kin
With that clamour, this cold, those changes-to-come from skies
   Now a stained-glass blue in the whiteness of the weather.

# On the Principle of Blowclocks
## Three-way Poem[1]

*The static forces*

not a ball of silver

*of a solid body*

but a ball of air

*and its material strength*

whose globed sheernesses

*derive from*

shine with a twofold glitter:

*not the quantity of mass:*

once with the dew and once

*an engineer would instance*

with the constituent bright threads

*rails or T beams, say*

of all its spokes

*four planes constructed to*

in a tense surface

*contain the same volume as*

in a solid cloud of stars

*four tons of mass*


# Clouds

How should the dreamer, on those slow
    Solidities, fix his wandering adagio,
Seizing, bone-frail, blown
    Through the diaphanous air of their patrols,
Shadows of fanfares, grails of melting snow?
    How can he hope to hold that white

[1] A reading should include (a) the italicized lines, (b) the unitalicized, (c) the whole as printed.

Opacity as it endures, advances,
    At a dream's length? Its strength
Confounds him with detail, his glance falls
    From ridge to ridge down the soft canyon walls,
And, fleece as it may seem, its tones
    And touch are not the fleece of dream,
But light and body, spaced accumulation
    The mind can take its purchase on:
Cloudshapes are destinies, and they
    Charging the atmosphere of a common day,
Make it the place of confrontation where
    The dreamer wakes to the categorical call
And clear cerulean trumpet of the air.


## *Words for the Madrigalist*

Look with the ears, said Orazio Vecchi,
    Trusting to music, willing to be led
Voluntarily blind through its complete
    Landscape of the emotion, feeling beneath the feet
Of the mind's heart, the land fall, the height
    Re-form: Look with the ears—they are all
Looking with the eyes, missing the way:
    So, waiting for sleep, I look
With the ears at the confused clear sounds
    As each replenished tributary unwinds
Its audible direction, and dividing
    The branchwork of chime and counterchime
Runs the river's thick and drumming stem:
    Loud with their madrigal of limestone beds
Where nothing sleeps, they all
    Give back—not the tune the listener calls
But the measure of what he is
    In the hard, sweet music of his lack,
The unpremeditated consonances: and the words
    Return it to you over the ground-
Bass of their syllables, Orazio Vecchi:
    Hear with the eyes as you catch the current of their sounds.

# Anecdote

Carlos Trujillo
killed this mountain wolf
that killed his calf,

and strung it
high on a pinebranch
below Mt. Lobo:

when I asked him, 'Why?—
for all the other
coyotes to see?'

his reply was:
'I did it
so the birds should have meat.'

*Kiowa Ranch*

# Arroyo Hondo

Twice I'd tried
to pass the
bastard outside
of Arroyo Hondo:
each time, the same
thing: out he
came in a
wobbling glide
in that beat-up
pick-up, his
head bent
in affable accompaniment,
jawing at
the guy who sat
beside him: the third
time (ready
for him) I
cut out wide,
flung him
a passing look as I
made it: we almost

171

made it together
he and I: the same
thing, out he
came, all crippled speed
unheeding: I could not
retreat and what
did I see? I
saw them
playing at cards
on the driving seat.

## The Matachines

Where, but here
would you
find—not
ten miles
from the city limit,
on an afternoon
graced by the feast-
day of Saint
Antony of Padua;
where, but here
all ranged
in a double line
masked as Moors
and dancing the morris
—the Moorish dance,
to the repetitions
of a high
fiddle and a low
guitar—where
but in this
play
of the way the Moors
were beaten in Spain,
that became
the story
in which Cortez
conquered
Moctezuma of Mexico
helped by his
Indian mistress

the Malinche: she
and the daughter
of the Moroccan emperor
(dual betrayal)
meet
in the white
minute girl
dancing in her
communion dress
between
the lines of men;
and where the bull
came from
nobody says
or why she
must betray
him too,
waving her
scarf of red
confusing his
tied-on horns,
his head
of a wrinkled
Spanish parishioner:
it is a
dance of
multiform confusions—
she
the Malinche
the Moorish bride
and the holy
Virgin all
in one:
conquistadores
all these
dressed-up Moors
before the saint,
and now, backwards
they dance to church,
the saint's
canopy carried
after them, until
by the door the double
line pause

and there the saint
passes in between them:
following, they
enter dancing
as if to say,
we are here
whatever we
do or
mean in this
dance
of the bull
and the betrayal:
whatever we
do we mean
as praise, praise
to the saint
and the occasion,
to the high
altar and its
ponderous crucifix
above: it is
done:
it is clear
the music
in the cool aisle
that the open
air dispersed:
we are here.

*San Antonio, New Mexico*


## Before the Dance

### at Zuni

The dance
is not yet
and when it will begin
no one says:
the waiting
for the Indian
is half the dance,
and so they wait

giving a quality
to the moment
by their refusal
to measure it:
the moment
is expansible
it burns
unconsumed
under the raw bulbs
of the dancing chamber:
the Navajo faces
wear
the aridity of the landscape
and 'the movement
with the wind
of the Orient and
the movement against
the wind
of the Occident'
meet
in their wrinkles:
they wait, sitting
(the moment)
on the earth floor
(is expansible)
saying very little
or sleep
like the woman
slipping along the wall
sideways
to wake
in the clangour of the pulse of time
at the beginning
drum . . .

## A Sense of Distance

The door is shut.
The red rider
no longer crosses the canyon floor
under a thousand feet of air.

The glance that fell
on him, is shafting
a deeper well:
the boughs of the oak are roaring
inside the acorn shell.

The hoofbeats—silent, then—
are sounding now
that ride
dividing a later distance.

For I am in England,
and the mind's embrace
catches-up this English
and that horizonless desert space
into its own, and the three there
concentrically fill a single sphere.

And it seems as if a wind
had flung wide a door
above an abyss, where all
the kingdoms of possibilities shone
like sandgrains crystalline in the mind's own sun.


## The Instance

They do say said
the barber running
his cold shears
downwards and over
the neck's sudden
surprised flesh:
They do say frost
will flow in
through the gap of a hedge
like water, and go
anywhere and I
believe it. I believe
him—a gardener,
he knows. The tepid
day erases
his wisdom and he

is out of mind
until at night
I grope for a way
between darkness and door
and passing a hand
down over
a parked car's
roof feel
the finger tips
burn at the crystal
proof of a frost
that finding a hole
in the hedge
has flowed through like water.


## A Little Night Music

A shimmer at the ear: a sheen
the all-but-done day
would still detain it with:
a dying hoard of
wholly-unseen-now,
just-heard visitations:
small sounds poise
superimpose, then shift
as lightly as summer-flies
go glinting down
the drift of late air cooling:
a spate of sibilances: a maze
in motion where the foursquare
frontier of tree girths, the million
leaves beating there, are
spread weed in sleep's underwater: a
wincing and wandering of evanescences:
a not-listening ear.

# The Awakening

The storm wind
was tearing at sleep: as it struck
a tremor through rafter and dream,
you might have been a rook
clinging in the swung tree.

Clear-cut, the canon beat on
beneath dark: the predictable
seashore simmer-then-crash as the flood
of air flung itself
into an uproar of woodland.

In here, out there—where
were you? You were
all at once awake. And it was not the storm
had lopped the branches of your dream
but the quiet: the wind had dropped.

What the pane now showed
was unquivering rainbuds loading
a rose-bare tangle of bush and, magnified
in the still, grey air of the lapse,
ponderous beech-boles, like silence solidified.

# The Windshield

You took it in
at a glance: the March
snow-clouds seemed to be dancing
as the gale impelled
their glittering reflections over the windshield.

No snow fell. A gusty sun
was switching the shadows off and on,
making the steepness a deeper blue
that the reflections were broken across
and sailing through. Your glance

gave back a sense of the force
contained by the framing glass;
so seen, crag and shelf
of the cloud grew exact in power,
for sky is sky and no measure of itself.

Under the roar of the black
veinwork of branches, the whole city lay
open to the illumination
that pierced between door and car-door
out of the random fierceness of season and day.


## Last Days of the Miser

An immaculate
December garden
of ranked cabbages
glows green
before his smoky door which stands
half-open: the room
behind it is a flue
the fume prefers
to the unswept chimney
and on the wall, a black
glass, or picture
it could be, is all
that hangs there.
Bread, cup and spoon
have drunk the same
impenetrable tone
at the lonely table,
along-side which he
sits, coloured like them.
He is crying
silently with the smoke,
as unaware of it
as of the tears
or what it is that works
his jaws unceasingly,
drawing his lost
look downwards.
His palate hoards

nothing, the irreducible
bolus, and the something
he still is, expends
all of its poor
power against it
swelling within him,
stopping his mouth
with the taste of time
wasted and of time
yet to be
gnawed small
to the same grist.

His mind's tooth
can find
less sustenance
than the mice
among his tattered notes
(has he forgone the recollection
even of them?).
An hour and more
I have been
sitting with him, before he
rouses to a stare and I
feed the silence
with That's a smoky
chimney you've got
in here. His reply
absently judicious,
slow to come—
I got, he says,
a smokier one at home,
which is where he is.


## Rumour

we called him—with his three
chins, earnest
of as many tongues,
and Rumour had it and Rumour
spread it that we
were moving away

because we'd sold the table:
Rumour could elevate
the bare stone of a truth into
the instant architecture of a fable.
Your duck is
serving was the word
he used, your goose:
I've been watching them
for an hour behind the house
said voyeur Rumour.
An hour? An hour.
Is it possible, I said
wondering at the result—
Possible, he replied
but difficult.
Deciding
to woo Circumstance
Rumour will come on
wearing the look of Indigence.
Sorry for him, I
offer strawberries from a basket:
You haven't a fag, he asks.
No. I haven't a fag,
so with a great
reluctance, he manages to eat
one of them. But with his
You can believe me,
I'm telling you no lie
it's not long before
he's laying claim
to his proper glory,
his own construction
put upon plain
fact, and launched
on a likely story
to exercise his chins
Rumour is Rumour once again.

# Terminal Tramps

The first is female.
In the station restaurant,
taking tea
that some thirsty traveller
had found too hot
for drinking, she sips
at the unmeasured time of her
terrible leisure.
The eyes of the mad
have a restless candour:
even their furtiveness
betrays itself openly:
there seems, in the way
she declares to the entire
room: *I expect
a civil answer*—
the appearance of an honesty.
It is distinct from the absurd
sobriety in the drunk
tramp's gesture
carrying on
in the corner, an imitation
conversation, with one
as craftily glanced as he
but sober. All
three inhabit
this shifting place
on whose fluidities the clocks
impose a certainty.
The room is aware of them.
The room is tolerant
in its curiosity and waits
to see, but to see
what? The Indian
personnel pretend
that the three are not
there—even the mad
woman has had
sense to avoid
in this two-roomed
restaurant, the white
management next-door.

What does occur
is this—this
and no more: she picks
out of the air and starts
to repeat the word
*Eisenhower*. She takes
apart into its four
syllables the arbitrary
sound, then feels
her way out
over them, as though
they might have led
her somewhere, stretched
from here to there,—
might have proved
there there, but the mind's
needle merely
chokes on its repetitions
until, with an accumulating
force, the vortex
spins her on
into inconsequence.
The drunk walks
suddenly half
the room's length,
balanced tensely
by the strength of one
determination—to make it;
and to complete the demonstration
he flings with a total
accuracy into the slot
of a litter bin
his emptied bottle.
Her babble stops him.
He attends, and for the first
time sees her:
she takes him in,
her din rises
raging against the mere
shape he makes there:
it is her voice not she
gets up to accost him
and to demand her civil
answer. Answer

she has, but whether
she hears, or whether
she can interpret
the sharp transition
as with half a threat
he gestures at her, then
lets the gesture
drift, die out across
the air ... with an
*Ach!*—the dawning
sense of her daftness—
he goes back
aiming himself at his former
corner, and gets
there on both
feet, as neat
as bottle into bin-slot—
to resume (he has clearly
forgotten her) his parody
of someone perfectly
self-possessed. The room
holding its breath
for his fall
is relieved. The room
has seen it all and now
inches out daughters
and sons into the loud
sane ambience
of train-sounds.
Under the dome
of stale air,
two Indians are
going their rounds,
swabbing the tables.
They circle the one
she sits at
with her all-but-spent
babble, her syllable-
chopping search
for the right sound,
the word to express
her groundless humanity,

hunched, alien
and intent amid
the new invasion
of travellers with a destination.


## The Fox Gallery

A long house—
the fox gallery you called
its upper storey, because
you could look down to see
(and did) the way a fox would
cross the field beyond
and you could follow out, window
to window, the fox's way
the whole length of the meadow
parallel with the restraining line
of wall and pane, or as far
as that could follow the sense of all
those windings. Do you remember
the morning I woke you with the cry
Fox fox and the animal
came on—not from side
to side, but straight
at the house and we craned
to see more and more, the most
we could of it and then
watched it sheer off deterred
by habitation, and saw
how utterly the two worlds were
disparate, as that perfect
ideogram for agility
and liquefaction flowed
away from us rhythmical
and flickering and
that flare was final.

# Frost

clings to the shadows, a wan silhouette
mapping out the house
in flat projection. Fields freeze still
under the hill's cold shoulder,
but winter cannot keep white
for long this shadowy frontier. Crowns
of rime (no reason to climb for them)
ring the under-oak grass, where one
by one the sunlight is melting them down.

# Composition

### for John Berger

Courbet might have painted this
gigantic head: heavy, yellow
petal-packed bloom of the chrysanthemum.

He would have caught the way
the weight of it looms from the cheap-green
vase this side the window it lolls in.

But he would have missed the space
triangled between stalk and curtain
along a window-frame base.

The opulence of the flower
would have compelled him to ignore
the ship-shape slotted verticals

of the door in the house beyond
dwarfed by the wand of the stem;
and the gate before it would not

have echoed those parallels to his eye
with its slatted wood, its two
neat side-posts of concrete.

The triangle compacts the lot: there
is even room in it for the black
tyre and blazing wheel-hub of a car

parked by the entrance. But the eye
of Courbet is glutted with petals
as solid as meat that press back the sky.


## The Beautiful Aeroplane

Under its hangar the afternoon
waits for a less brilliant time,
a time of less dry sunlight
on shapes grown uncertain.

The nailheads of the first flowers
will be rustier then, the coming
grass ground-out under the treads
of the speculator's assistant

as he moves on down the first
hill and the next, his yellow
bulldozer arbitrarily cheerful
where now there can be

no confusion in sequence
as you pass between
the spaced-out parts—they
that a touch might slide together

and the wing united to the fuselage
the balancing tail tower, a high
axis between and above
the articulate shining assembly.


## To be Engraved
## on the Skull of a Cormorant

across the thin
façade, the galleried-
with-membrane head:
narrowing, to take
the eye-dividing
declivity where

the beginning beak
prepares for flight
in a still–
perfect salience:
here, your glass
needs must stay
steady and your gross
needle re-tip
itself with reticence
but be
as searching as the sea
that picked and pared
this head yet spared
its frail acuity.

## Gull

### for Louis and Celia

Flung
far down,
as the
gull rises,
the black
smile of
its shadow
masking its
underside
takes
the heart
into the height
to hover
above the ocean's
plain-of-mountains'
moving quartz.

# *Oppositions*[1]

### debate with Mallarmé
### for Octavio Paz

The poet must rescue etymology from among the footnotes, thus moving up into the body of the text, '*cipher:* the Sanskrit word *sunya* derived from the root *svi*, to swell.'

To cipher is to turn the thought word into flesh. And hence 'the body of the text' derives its substance.

The master who disappeared, taking with him into the echo-chamber the ptyx which the Styx must replenish, has left the room so empty you would take it for fullness.

Solitude charges the house. If all is mist beyond it, the island of daily objects within becomes clarified.

Mistlines flow slowly in, filling the land's declivity that lay unseen until that indistinctness had acknowledged them.

If the skull is a memento mori, it is also a room, whose contained space is wordlessly resonant with the steps that might cross it, to command the vista out of its empty eyes.

Nakedness can appear as the vestment of space that separates four walls, the flesh as certain then and as transitory as the world it shares.

The mind is a hunter of forms, binding itself, in a world that must decay, to present substance.

Skull and shell, both are helmeted, both reconcile vacancy with its opposite. *Abolis bibelots d'inanité sonore.* Intimate presences of silent plenitude.

# *Autumn*

The civility of nature overthrown, the badger must fight in the roofless colosseum of the burning woods.

The birds are in flight, and the sky is in flight, raced by as many clouds as there are waves breaking the lakes beneath it.

Does Tristan lie dying, starred by the oak leaves? Tristan is on horseback, in search, squat, with narrow eyes, saddleless, burner of cities.

[1] 'Oppositions' replies to one of Mallarmé's most famous sonnets, '*Ses purs ongles très haut dédiant leur onyx*', whose '*ptyx*' is explained as being a sea shell.

The field mouse that fled from the blade, flattened by wheels, has dried into the shape of a leaf, a minute paper escutcheon whose tail is the leaf stalk.

Yet the worm still gathers its rings together and releases them into motion ... You too must freeze.

The horses of Attila scatter the shed foliage under the splashed flags of a camp in transit.

A truce: the first rime has not etched the last oak-shocks; the rivermist floats back from the alders and the sun pauses there.

Peace? There will be no peace until the fragility of the mosquito is overcome and the spirals of the infusoria turn to glass in the crystal pond.

These greens are the solace of lakes under a sun which corrodes. They are memorials not to be hoarded.

There will be a truce, but not the truce of the rime with the oak leaf, the mist with the alders, the rust with the sorrel stalk or of the flute with cold.

It will endure? It will endure as long as the frost.

## Tout Entouré de Mon Regard

Surrounded by your glance—shapes at the circumference of its half-circle staring back into foreground shapes—, you measure the climbing abyss up to the birds that intersect in contrary directions the arc of winter air.

To the question you did not ask, comes the reply of arriving and departing cloud, the intensifying violet skyline that throws forward its patterns of boughs, the spaces between them flushed with a glowing obscurity.

It is like a phalanx of moth-wings with their separations of line and darkly incandescent tints, pressed against a window which is no window and behind which, burning towards them, a late sun hangs.

Surrounded by your glance, you are the pivot of that scale half of which balances in darkness behind you. And you feel its insistence held over against the light, the yellowing sky, the colliding of imitation mountains that presage more snow.

To see, is to feel at your back this domain of a circle whose power consists in evading and refusing to be completed by you.

It is infinity sustains you on its immeasurable palm.

# Skullshapes

Skulls. Finalities. They emerge towards new beginnings from under-growth. Along with stones, fossils, flint keel-scrapers and spoke-shaves, along with bowls of clay pipes heel-stamped with their makers' marks, comes the rural detritus of cattle skulls brought home by children. They are moss-stained, filthy with soil. Washing them of their mottlings, the hand grows conscious of weight, weight sharp with jaggednesses. Suspend them from a nail and one feels the bone-clumsiness go out of them: there is weight still in their vertical pull downwards from the nail, but there is also a hanging fragility. The two qualities fuse and the brush translates this fusion as wit, where leg-like appendages conclude the skulls' dangling mass.

Shadow explores them. It sockets the eye-holes with black. It reaches like fingers into the places one cannot see. Skulls are a keen instance of this duality of the visible: it borders what the eye cannot make out, it transcends itself with the suggestion of all that is there beside what lies within the eyes' possession: it cannot be possessed. Flooded with light, the skull is at once manifest surface and labyrinth of recesses. Shadow reaches down out of this world of helmeted cavities and declares it.

One sees. But not merely the passive mirrorings of the retinal mosaic—nor, like Ruskin's blind man struck suddenly by vision, without memory or conception. The senses, reminded by other seeings, bring to bear on the act of vision their pattern of images; they give point and place to an otherwise naked and homeless impression. It is the mind sees. But what it sees consists not solely of that by which it is confronted grasped in the light of that which it remembers. It sees possibility.

The skulls of birds, hard to the touch, are delicate to the eye. Egg-like in the round of the skull itself and as if the spherical shape were the result of an act like glass-blowing, they resist the eyes' imaginings with the blade of the beak which no lyrical admiration can attenuate to frailty.

The skull of nature is recess and volume. The skull of art—of possibility—is recess, volume and also lines—lines of containment, lines of extension. In seeing, one already extends the retinal impression, searchingly and instantaneously. Brush and pen extend the search beyond the instant, touch discloses a future. Volume, knived across by the challenge of a line, the raggedness of flaking bone countered by ruled, triangular facets, a cowskull opens a visionary field, a play of universals.

# The Daisies

All evening, daisies outside the window, have gone on flying, stalk-anchored, towards the dark. Still, vibrant, swaying, they have stood up through dryness into beating rain: stellar cutouts, arrested explosions; too papery thin to be 'flower-heads'—flower-faces perhaps; upturned hands with innumerable fingers. Unlike the field daisies, they do not shut with dark: they stretch as eagerly towards it as they did to the sun, images of flight. And your own image, held by the pane, diffuses your features among those of the daisies, so that you flow with them until your hand, lifted to close the window, becomes conscious of its own heaviness. It is their stalks thrust them into flight as much as their launching-out of winged fingers, all paper accents, *grave* thrusting on acute, acute on *grave*. Cut the stalks and they fall, they do not fly; let them lose their bond and they, too, would grow, not lighter, but suddenly heavy with the double pull of their flower flesh and of the rain clinging to them.

# Poem

The muscles which move the eyeballs, we are told, derive from a musculature which once occupied the body end to end ... Sunblaze as day goes, and the light blots back the scene to iris the half-shut lashes. A look can no longer extricate the centre of the skyline copse. But the last greys, the departing glows caught by the creepers bearding its mass, prevail on the half-blinded retina. Branches deal with the air, vibrating the beams that thread into one's eye. So that 'over there' and 'in here' compound a truce neither signed—a truce that, insensibly and categorically, grows to a decree, and what one hoped for and what one is, must measure themselves against those demands which the eye receives, delivering its writ on us through a musculature which occupies the body end to end.

# Ceci n'est pas une Pipe[1]
### (Magritte)

This is not a pipe, but an explosion of the lips, the mouth unseaming rapidly and the lips exploding once more.

---

[1] '*Ceci n'est pas une pipe*' is the caption to a painting of a pipe—one that you smoke, not play—by Magritte.

This is not only a statement. It has roots. And they are unpleasant, as though the possibility distinctly existed that lips should explode without benefit of quotation marks.

Our words surround us with contingencies. The mouth unseaming rapidly may do so like an unstitched wound. This is not a pipe.

We summon our terrors before us, to cohabit with clocks, plants, window-panes and apples, as if we would always know the worst.

But we are scarcely to be trusted. Our 'sinnes of fear' remain as incorrigible as our groundless optimisms.

So we terrorize ourselves factitiously, with the body that has become a face, or the face that has become a body. But 'this is not a pipe'.

Such a face disproves itself. It could terrorize only by existing.

There is this comfort in the hypotheses of fancy: they restore the world to us by denying its premises.

This is not a stone because it is flying. This is not a bird because it is made of stone.

Yet the flying stone impends over the landscape by abstracting all the qualities of the real one. And the density of the stone bird is negated by the contours of flight.

This is not a pipe, but it entails the rider that the stone will interpose an irremovable 'and yet—', and the bird spread wings of bone and feather towards its point of high vantage.

## A Process

A process; procession; trial.

A process of weather, a continuous changing. Thus, the gloom before darkness engenders its opposite and snow begins. Or rain possesses the night unbrokenly from the dazzle on the lit streets to the roar, dense, ubiquitous and incessant, that overcomes the hills drinking-in their black harvest. Its perfect accompaniment would be that speech of islanders, in which, we are told, the sentence is never certainly brought to an end, its aim less to record with completeness the impression an event makes, than to mark its successive aspects as they catch the eye, the ear of the speaker.

To process: to walk the bounds to lay claim to them, knowing all they exclude.

A procession, a body of things proceeding, as in the unending commerce of cloud with the seamless topology of the ground. Or a

193

procession of waters: the whole moving belt of it swallows itself in sudden falls to be regurgitated as combed-over foam. Flung in reverse against the onrush that immediately pushes it forward, it is replaced by its own metamorphosis into this combed-back whiteness.

A trial: the whole of the proceedings, including the complication and the unravelling. One accords the process its reality, one does not deify it; inserted among it, one distinguishes and even transfigures, so that the quality of vision is never a prisoner of the thing seen. The beginnings have to be invented: thus the pictograph is an outline, which nature, as the poet said, does not have. And the ends? The ends are windows opening above that which lay unperceived until the wall of the house was completed at that point, over that sea.

## The Chances of Rhyme

The chances of rhyme are like the chances of meeting—
    In the finding fortuitous, but once found, binding:
They say, they signify and they succeed, where to succeed
    Means not success, but a way forward
If unmapped, a literal, not a royal succession;
    Though royal (it may be) is the adjective or region
That we, nature's royalty, are led into.
    Yes. We are led, though we seem to lead
Through a fair forest, an Arden (a rhyme
    For Eden)—breeding ground for beasts
Not bestial, but loyal and legendary, which is more
    Than nature's are. Yet why should we speak
Of art, of life, as if the one were all form
    And the other all Sturm-und-Drang? And I think
Too, we should confine to Crewe or to Mow
    Cop, all those who confuse the fortuitousness
Of art with something to be met with only
    At extremity's brink, reducing thus
Rhyme to a kind of rope's end, a glimpsed grass
    To be snatched at as we plunge past it—
Nostalgic, after all, for a hope deferred.
    To take chances, as to make rhymes
Is human, but between chance and impenitence
    (A half-rhyme) come dance, vigilance
And circumstance (meaning all that is there
    Besides you, when you are there). And between

Rest-in-peace and precipice,
    Inertia and perversion, come the varieties
Increase, lease, re-lease (in both
    Senses); and immersion, conversion—of inert
Mass, that is, into energies to combat confusion.
    Let rhyme be my conclusion.


# The End

All those who have not died have married.
    A Pompeian pause arrests
Merton beside his window, and the view
    Below is parkland, final as none
Could be, but the moment after she
    Whose name is on the card he holds
Has gone. The sliver of pasteboard framed
    By the great window, now, forever,
He is perfected in regret. Dalton
    Hailing the cab that will carry him
Out of the book, the motif on his lips
    (*So much for London, then*) for the last time,
The last chord chimes, tolling the solitudes
    Of the vast mind they moved in.
Such ends are just. But let him know
    Who reads his time by the way books go,
Each instant will bewry his symmetries
    And Time, climbing down from its pedestal
Uncrown the settled vista of his loss.
    Is it autumn or spring? It is autumn or spring.
Before door and window, the terrible guest
    Towers towards a famine and a feast.

# WRITTEN ON WATER
## (1972)

# On Water

'Furrow' is inexact:
no ship could be
converted to a plough
travelling this vitreous ebony:

seal it in sea-caves and
you cannot still it:
image on image bends
where half-lights fill it

with illegible depths
and lucid passages,
bestiary of stones,
book without pages:

and yet it confers
as much as it denies:
we are orphaned and fathered
by such solid vacancies:

# Mackinnon's Boat

Faced to the island, Mackinnon's boat
  Arcs out: the floats of his creels
Cling to the shelter half a mile away
  Of Tarner's cliff. Black, today
The waters will have nothing to do with the shaping
  Or unshaping of human things. No image
Twists beside the riding launch, there to repeat
  Its white and blue, its unrigged mast
Slanting from the prow in which a dog
  Now lies stretched out—asleep
It seems, but holds in steady view
  Through all-but-closed eyes the grey-black
Water travelling towards it. The surface,
  Opaque as cliffstone, moves scarred
By a breeze that strikes against its grain
  In ruffled hatchings. Distance has disappeared,
Washed out by mist, but a cold light
  Keeps here and there re-touching it,

Promising transparencies of green and blue
　　Only to deny them. The visible sea
Remains a sullen frontier to
　　Its unimaginable fathoms. The dog eyes
Its gliding shapes, but the signs he can recognize
　　Are land signs: he is here
Because men are here, unmindful
　　Of this underworld of Mackinnon's daily dealings.
As the creels come in, he'll lie
　　Still watching the waters, nostrils
Working on seasmells, but indifferent
　　To the emerging haul, clawed and crawling.
The cliff lifts near, and a guttural cry
　　Of cormorants raises his glance: he stays
Curled round on himself: his world
　　Ignores this waste of the in-between,
Air and rock, stained, crag-sheer
　　Where cormorants fret and flock
Strutting the ledges. The two men
　　Have sited their destination. Mackinnon
Steering, cuts back the engine and Macaskill
　　Has the light floats firm and then
The weight of the freighted creels is on his rope—
　　A dozen of them—the coil spitting
Water as it slaps and turns on the windlass
　　Burning Macaskill's palms paying it in.
As the cold, wet line is hauled, the creels
　　Begin to arrive. And, inside, the flailing
Seashapes pincered to the baits, drop
　　Slithering and shaken off like thieves
Surprised, their breath all at once grown rare
　　In an atmosphere they had not known existed.
Hands that have much to do yet, dealing
　　With creel on creel, drag out the catch
And feeling the cage-nets, re-thread each fault.
　　Crabs, urchins, dogfish, and star,
All are unwanted and all are
　　Snatched, slaughtered, or flung to their freedom—
Some, shattering on the cordage
　　They too eagerly clung to. Hands must be cruel
To keep the pace spry to undo and then
　　To re-tie, return the new-baited traps
To water, but an ease makes one
　　The disparate links of the concerted action

Between the first drawing in
  And the let down crash of stone-weighted baskets.
There is more to be done still. The trough of the gunwhale
  Is filled with the scrabbling armour of defeat;
Claw against claw, not knowing
  What it is they fight, they swivel
And bite on air until they feel
  The palpable hard fingers of their real
Adversary close on them; and held
  In a knee-grip, must yield to him.
The beaked claws are shut and bound
  By Mackinnon. Leaning against the tiller,
He impounds each one alive
  In the crawling hatch. And so the boat
Thrusts on, to go through a hundred and more creels
  Before the return. Macaskill throws
To Mackinnon a cigarette down the length
  Of half the craft. Cupping,
They light up. Their anonymity, for a spell,
  Is at an end, and each one
Free to be himself once more
  Sharing the rest that comes of labour.
But labour must come of rest: and already
  They are set towards it, and soon the floats
Of the next creel-drift will rise
  Low in the water. An evasive light
Brightens like mist rolling along the sea,
  And the blue it beckoned—blue
Such as catches and dies in an eye-glance—
  Glints out its seconds. Making a time
Where no day has a name, the smells
  Of diesel, salt, and tobacco mingle:
They linger down a wake whose further lines
  Are beginning to slacken and fall back to where
Salt at last must outsavour name and time
  In the alternation of the forgetful waters.

                                        *Ullinish*

# The Thief's Journal

'Only this book of love will be real. What of the facts which served as its pretext? I must be their repository'. GENET

How much there was had escaped him:
The suns were outpacing his vagrancy:
He had crossed Andalusia. Andalusia
Was what it was still to be
Without him. It tantalized imagination
The taste of the fish he had eaten there without salt or bread
At his sea-wrack fire whose ashes
The careful sea had long-since appropriated.

## Rower

A plotless tale: the passing hours
  Bring in a day that's nebulous. Glazes of moist pearl
Mute back the full blaze of a sea,
  Drifting continually where a slack tide
Has released the waters. Shallows
  Spread their transparency, letting through
A pale-brown map of sandbanks
  Barely submerged, where a gull might wade
Thin legs still visible above its blurred reflection.
  It seems nothing will occur here until
The tide returns, ferrying to the shore its freshness,
  Beating and breaking only to remake itself
The instant the advancing line goes under.
  And nothing does. Except for the inching transformations
Of a forenoon all melting redundancies
  Just beyond eyeshot: the grey veils
Drink-in a little more hidden sunlight,
  Shadows harden, pale. But then
Out into the bay, towards deeper water,
  Sidles the rower, gaining speed
As he reaches it. Already his world
  Is sliding by him. Backwards
He enters it, eyes searching the past
  Before them: that shape that crowns the cliff,
A sole, white plane, draws tight his gaze—
  A house, bereft so it seems of time

By its place of vantage, high
  Over cleft and crack. When, as momentarily,
He steals a glance from it to fling
  Across his travelling shoulder, his eyes
Soon settle once more along that line
  Tilted towards the shoremark. And though the ripple
Is beneath him now—the pull and beat
  Unfelt when further in—he cuts athwart it
Making his way, to the liquid counterpulse
  Of blades that draw him outwards to complete
The bay's half-circle with his own. Muscle
  And bone work to that consummation of the will
Where satisfaction gathers to surfeit, strain
  To ease. Pleased by his exertions, he abandons them
Riding against rested oars, subdued
  For the moment to that want of purpose
In sky and water, before he shoots
  Feathering once more baywards, his face
To the direction the tide will take when
  Out of the coherent chaos of a morning that refuses
To declare itself, it comes plunging in
  Expunging the track of his geometries.


## The Lighthouse

The lighthouse is like the church of some island sect
  Who have known the mainland beliefs and have defected
Only to retain them in native purity
  And in the daily jubilation of storm and sea,
But adding every day new images
  To their liturgy of changes—each one
Some myth over and done with now
  Because sea has rebegotten land and land
The sea, and all is waiting to declare
  That things have never been praised for what they were, emerging
Along promontory on enfiladed promontory.

# Two Poems on titles proposed by Octavio and Marie José Paz

## I. Le Rendez-Vous des Paysages

The promenade, the plage, the paysage
all met somewhere
in the reflection of a reflection
in midair: cars, unheard,
were running on water: jetplanes
lay on their backs
like sunbathers
in a submarine graveyard
about to resurrect into the fronds
of ghost-palms boasting
'We exist'
to the sea's uncertain mirrors
to the reversed clocktowers that had lost
all feeling for time
suspended
among the overlapping vistas
of promenade, plage, paysage.

## II. La Promenade de Protée

Changing, he walks the changing avenue:
this blue and purple are the blue
and purple of autumn underwater:
they are changing to green and he
is changing to an undulated statue
in this sea-floor park
and does not know
if the iced green will undo him
or which are real
among the recollections that cling
to him and seem to know him:
and hears overhead the shudder of departing keels.

# Stone Speech

Crowding this beach
are milkstones, white
teardrops; flints
edged out of flinthood
into smoothness chafe
against grainy ovals,
pitted pieces, nosestones,
stoppers and saddles;
veins of orange
inlay black beads:
chalk-swaddled babyshapes,
tiny fists, facestones
and facestone's brother
skullstone, roundheads
pierced by a single eye,
purple finds, all
rubbing shoulders:
a mob of grindings,
groundlings, scatterings
from a million necklaces
mined under sea-hills, the pebbles
are as various as the people.


# The Sea is Open to the Light

The sea is open to the light:
the image idling
beneath the skerry
is the unmoving
skerry's own
rockbound foundation
travelling down and down
to meet in the underdeeps
the spread floor
shadowed where the fish
flash in their multitude
transmitting and eluding
the illumination.

# Variation on Paz

*Hay que . . . soñar hacia dentro y tambien hacia afuera*

We must dream inwards, and we must dream
   Outwards too, until—the dream's ground
Bound no longer by the dream—we feel
   Behind us the sea's force, and the blind
Keel strikes gravel, grinding
   Towards a beach where, eye by eye,
The incorruptible stones are our witnessess
   And we wake to what is dream and what is real
Judged by the sun and the impartial sky.


# The Compact: at Volterra

The crack in the stone, the black filament
   Reaching into the rockface unmasks
More history than Etruria or Rome
   Bequeathed this place. The ramparted town
Has long outlived all that; for what
   Are Caesar or Scipio beside
The incursion of the slow abyss, the daily
   Tribute the dry fields provide

Trickling down? There is a compact
   To undo the spot, between the unhurried sun
Edging beyond this scene, and the moon,
   Risen already, that has stained
Through with its pallor the remaining light:
   Unreal, that clarity of lips and wrinkles
Where shadow investigates each fold,
   Scaling the cliff to the silhouetted stronghold.

Civic and close-packed, the streets
   Cannot ignore this tale of unshorable earth
At the town brink; furrow, gully,
   And sandslide guide down
Each seeping rivulet only to deepen
   The cavities of thirst, dry out
The cenozoic skeleton, appearing, powdering away,
   Uncovering the chapped clay beneath it.

There is a compact between the cooling earth
    And every labyrinthine fault that mines it—
The thousand mouths whose language
    Is siftings, whisperings, rumours of downfall
That might, in a momentary unison,
    Silence all, tearing the roots of sound out
With a single roar: but the cicadas
    Chafe on, grapevine entwines the pergola

Gripping beyond itself. A sole farm
    Eyes space emptily. Those
Who abandoned it still wire
    Their vines between lopped willows:
Their terraces, fondling the soil together,
    Till up to the drop that which they stand to lose:
Refusing to give ground before they must,
    They pit their patience against the dust's vacuity.

The crack in the stone, the black filament
    Rooting itself in dreams, all live
At a truce, refuted, terracing; as if
    Unreasoned care were its own and our
Sufficient reason, to repair the night's derisions,
    Repay the day's delight, here where the pebbles
Of half-ripe grapes abide their season,
    Their fostering leaves outlined by unminding sky.

# Two Poems of Lucio Piccolo

## I. Unstill Universe

    Unstill universe of gusts
of rays, of hours without colour, of perennial
transits, vain displays
of cloud: an instant and—
look, the changed forms
blaze out, milennia grow unstable.
    And the arch of the low door and the step
worn by too many winters, are a fable
in the unforeseen burst from the March sun.

## II. Veneris Venefica Agrestis

She springs from the ground-clinging thicket, her face
—gay now, now surly—bound in a black
kerchief, a shrivelled chestnut it seems: no fine fleece
the hair that falls loose, but a lock
of curling goat-hair; when she goes by
(is she standing or bending?) her gnarled and dark
foot is a root that suddenly juts from the earth and walks.

    Be watchful she does not offer you her cup of bark,
its water root-flavoured that tastes of the viscid leaf,
either mulberry or sorb-apple, woodland fruit that flatters with lies
the lips but the tongue ties.

    She governs it seems
the force of rounding moons
that swells out the rinds of trees
and alternates the invincible ferments,
flow of the sap and of the seas . . .

    Pronubial, she, like the birds that bring
seeds from afar: arcane
the breeds that come of her grafting.

    And the mud walls of the unstable
cottage where the nettle grows
with gigantic stalk, are her realms of shadows:
she ignites the kindlings in the furnaces of fable.

    And round the door, from neighbouring orchard ground
the fumes that rise
are the fine, unwinding muslins of her sibiline vespers.

    She appears in the guise
of the centipede among the darknesses
by water-wheels that turn
no more in the maidenhair fern.

    She is the mask that beckons
and disappears, when the light
of the halfspent wicks
makes voracious the shadows in the room where
they are milling by night, working at the presses,
and odours of crushed olives are in the air,
kindled vapours of grapejuice; and lanterns come
swayed to the steps of hobnailed boots.

    The gestures of those who labour
in the fields, are accomplices
in the plots she weaves:
the stoop of those who gather up dry leaves

and acorns . . . and the shoeless tread and measured bearing
under burdened head, when you cannot see
the brow or the olives of the eyes
but only the lively mouth . . . the dress
swathes tight the flanks, the breasts, and has comeliness—
passing the bough she leaves behind
an odour of parching . . .
or the gesture that raises the crock
renewed at the basin of the spring.
    She bends, drawing a circle:
her sign sends forth
the primordial torrent out of the fearful earth
(and the foot that presses the irrigated furrow
and the hand that lifts
the spade—power of a different desire summons them now);
she draws strength
from the breaths of the enclosures,
the diffused cries, the damp and burning
straw of the litters, the blackened
branches of the vine, and the shadow that gives back
the smell of harnesses of rope and sack,
damp baskets, where who stands
on the threshold can descry
the stilled millstone, hoes long used to the grip of rural hands:
the rustic shade ferments with ancestral longings.
    Rockroses, thistles, pulicaria, calaminths—scents
that seem fresh and aromatic, are
(should your wariness pall) the lures
of a spiral that winds-in all,
(night bites into silver
free of all alloy of sidereal ray) she will
blur in a fume of dust the gentle hill-curve.
    Now, she's in daylight, one hand against an oak,
the other hangs loose — filthy and coaxing,
her dress black as a flue-brush . . .
and the sudden rush of wind
over the headland, sets at large
and floods with blue
a tangle of leaves and flourishing bough.
She promises, too, discloses the ardour,
freshness, vigour of the breath that frees
peach and the bitter-sweet
odour of the flowering almond tree; under coarse leaf
are fleshy and violent mouths, wild offshoots,

between the ferns' long fans
obscure hints of mushroom growths,
uncertain glances of water glint through the clovers,
and a sense of bare
original clay is there
near where the poplar wakes unslakeable thirst
with its rustling mirages of streams
and makes itself a mirror of each breeze,
where, in the hill's shade,
steep sloping,
the valley grows
narrow and closes
in the mouth of a spring
among delicate mosses.
   If, for a moment,
cloud comes to rest
over the hill-crest or the valley threshold,
in the living shade
the shaft of that plough now shows
which shakes which unflowers unleafs
the bush and the forest rose.

## At Sant' Antimo

Flanking the place,
a cypress
stretches itself, its surface
working as the wind
travels it in a continual
breathing, an underwater
floating of foliage
upwards, till
compact and wavering
it flexes a sinuous
tip that chases
its own shadow
to and fro
across the still
stone tower.

# Tarquinia

*Vince Viet Cong!* The testimony of walls.
What do they mean—'is winning'
Or 'let win'? In the beginning Tarquinia
Lorded ten provinces and has come to this,
A museum of tombstones, a necropolis.
Walls built of walls, the run-down
Etruscan capital is a town
Of bars and butchers' shops
Inside the wreck of palaces.
The Tomb of the Warriors. They are painted there
Carousing, drinking to victory. Said Forster,
'Let yourself be crushed.' They fought and were.
A woman goes past, bent by the weight
Of the trussed fowl she is trailing. The cross
Swings from her neck in accompaniment.
The eyes of the winged horses
That rode on the citadel are still keen
With the intelligence of a lost art.
*Vince Viet Cong!* What is it they mean?

# Santa Maria delle Nevi

Santa Maria
stands open
to the heat, a cave
of votive flames
that lure the eye
into the gloom
surrounding them. Lost
at first, one looks
for the ground and closure
to that fresh recess,
shallowly tunnelled-out
between its walls
and, in the end,
grasps it is the white
of painted snow
irradiates the altar-piece :
from bowl and salver
it overflows,
in snowballs like fruit,

an offering to
the Madonna of the Snows
and to the child
whom her restraining hands
hold steady,
its fingers curious
at the inexplicable
intimation of the cold:
an August dream,
and so exactly
does it fit the day
it seems to tally
with its opposite
in strength of fact,
where Santa Maria
hoards up the glow
of winter recollected
and summer inlays the street
as bright as snow.

## The Square

A consolidation
of voices in the street
below, a wave
that never reaches
its destination: the higher
voices of children
ride it and the raucous
monomaniac bikes
hunting their shadows
into the sunlight of the square
to a drum-roll
of metal shutters
sliding: and above it all
the reflection
hung on the open
pane (it opens
inwards) of the bell
over Santa Maria delle Nevi,
not even slightly
swung in the hot
evening air.

# Ariadne and the Minotaur[1]

When Theseus went down
she stood alone surrounded
by the sense of what finality it was
she entered now: the hot rocks offered her
neither resistance nor escape, but ran
viscous with the image of betrayal:
the pitted and unimaginable face
the minotaur haunted her with
kept forming there
along the seams and discolorations
and in the diamond sweat
of mica: the sword and thread
had been hers to give, and she
had given them, to this easer of destinies:
if she had gone
alone out of the sun and down where he
had threaded the way for her,
if she had gone
winding the ammonite of space
to where at the cold heart
from the dark stone the bestial warmth
would rise to meet her
unarmed in acquiescence, unprepared
her spindle of packthread . . . her fingers felt now
for the image in the sunlit rock, and her ears
at the shock of touch took up a cry
out of the labyrinth
into their own, a groaning
that filled the stone mouth
hollowly: between the lips of stone
appeared he whom she had sent
to go where her unspeakable
intent unspoken had been to go
herself, and heaved unlabyrinthed at her feet
their mutual completed crime—
a put-by destiny, a dying
look that sought her
out of eyes the light extinguished,

[1] Suggested initially by Picasso's series of drawings, this ignores as they do the question of
the actual kinship between Ariadne and the Minotaur. Perhaps she, too, was unaware of it.

eyes she should have led
herself to light: and the rays
that turned to emptiness in them
filling the whole of space with loss,
a waste of irrefutable sunlight spread
from Crete to Naxos.

## Machiavelli in Exile

A man is watching down the sun. All day,
Exploring the stone sinew of the hills,
For his every predilection it has asked
A Roman reason of him. And he has tried
To give one, tied to a dwindling patrimony
And the pain of exile. His guileless guile,
Trusted by nobody, he is self-betrayed.

And yet, for all that, Borgia shall be praised
Who moved and, moving, saved by sudden action:
The Florentines, despite their words, will have
Faction and the blood that comes of faction:
The work of France and Spain others begin—
Let him who says so exercise his powers
With dice and backgammon at a country inn;

Where, for his day's companions, he must choose
Such men as endure history and not those
Who make it: with their shadows, magnified
And spread behind them, butcher, publican,
Miller, and baker quarrel at their cards,
And heights and hill-roads all around are filled
With voices of gods who do not know they're gods.

Nor are they, save for a trick of light and sound:
Their fate is bound by their own sleeping wills.
Though lateness shadows all that's left to do,
*Tarde non furon mai grazie divine:*[1]
The sun that lit his mind now lights the page
At which he reads and words, hard-won, assuage
What chance and character have brought him to.

[1] *Tarde non furon mai grazie divine* (Divine graces were never late) is Machiavelli's misquotation of Petrarch's *Ma tarde non fur mai grazie divine*. It begins the letter to Francesco Vettori on which this poem is, in part, based.

He enters that courtly ancient company
Of men whose reasons may be asked, and he,
Released from tedium, poverty, and threat,
Lives in the light of possibility:
Their words are warm with it, yet tempered by
The memory of its opposite, else too soon
Hopes are a mob that wrangle for the moon.

Adversity puts his own pen in hand,
First torture, then neglect bringing to bear
The style and vigilance which may perfect
A prince, that he whom history forsook
Should for no random principle forsake
Its truth's contingency, his last defeat
And victory, no battle, but a book.


# *Hawks*

Hawks hovering, calling to each other
   Across the air, seem swung
Too high on the risen wind
   For the earth-clung contact of our world:
And yet we share with them that sense
   The season is bringing in, of all
The lengthening light is promising to exact
   From the obduracy of March. The pair,
After their kind are lovers and their cries
   Such as lovers alone exchange, and we
Though we cannot tell what it is they say,
   Caught up into their calling, are in their sway,
And ride where we cannot climb the steep
   And altering air, breathing the sweetness
Of our own excess, till we are kinned
   By space we never thought to enter
On capable wings to such reaches of desire.

# Of Beginning Light

The light of the mind is poorer
than beginning light: the shades
we find pigment for
poor beside the tacit
variety we can all see
yet cannot say: of beginning light
I will say this, that it dispenses
imperial equality to everything
it touches, so that purple
becomes common wear, but purple
resolving in its chord
a thousand tones
tinged by a thousand
shadows, all
yielding themselves
slowly up: and the mind,
feeling its way among
such hesitant distinctions,
is left behind as they
flare into certainties that
begin by ending them
in the light of day.

# Carscape

Mirrored
the rear window
holds a glowing
almost-gone-day
scene, although the day
across this upland
has far to go: one drives
against its glare
that by degrees a moving
Everest of cloud
will shadow-over
while amid these
many vanishings
replenished, the wintry
autumnal afternoon
could still be dawn.

# Drive

First light strikes
across a landmass
daylight hides: horizon
rides above horizon
momentarily
like a region of cloud:
I return driving
to the same view undone:
the windscreen takes it in
as a high and brilliant
emptiness that lies to one
of no depth, stretched above
palpabilities morning could touch:
and one feels for the features of the lost
continent (it seems)
of day's beginnings, recollection
seizing on the mind
with what infinity of unmarked
mornings, of spaces unsounded
habit abjures, in the cross-
tides of chaos, till we
believe our eyes (our lies)
that there is nothing there
but what we see—
and drive


# Legend

Midas eyes the seasonable glints:
    Pennywise, he hears the cash-crop
Clashing its foliage under the wind,
    As the buzz-saw in his mind
Bores through the pastoral irrelevance:
    Seen from this vantage, every view
Becomes a collector's item, and the atmosphere
    Squares off each parcel of bright worth
In bounding it: limbs to matchwood,
    Skyline saw-toothed to raw angles
Roof on roof, as Midas
    Stares the future into being, melts down

Season into season, past distinction,
    While the leaves too slowly
Deal their lightness to the air that lifts
    Then releases them on suppled boughs,
Time present beyond all bargain, liquid gifts.


## *Autumn Piece*

Baffled
by the choreography of the season
the eye could not
with certainty see
whether it was wind
stripping the leaves or
the leaves were struggling to be free:

They came at you
in decaying spirals
plucked flung and regathered by the same
force that was twisting
the scarves of the vapour trails
dragging all certainties out of course:

As the car resisted it
you felt it in either hand
commanding car, tree, sky,
master of chances,
and at a curve was a red
board said 'Danger':
I thought it said dancer.


## *The White Van*

new coated
a winter white
rides on ahead
through the brightness of
late autumn weather,
as the low and rising
side sun
flings from hedgerow

and from sky on to
its moving screen
a shadow show:
trees, half-unleafed,
fretted and pierced now
by sudden skylights,
come dancing down,
angle and mass and bough,
birds drawing them together
in their reflected flight:
this is all shape
and surface, you might say,
this black and white
abstraction of a coloured
day, but here
is no form so far
from what we see
it does not take the glow
and urgency of all
those goings-on
surrounding us: chance
unblinds certitude
with a fourth eye (the third
one is the mind's),
the paint of autumn
showing the more intense
for these pied
anatomies and
as the white van turns
right, distance
ahead of us
re-opens its density
of gold, green, amethyst.


## In October

A weather of flashes, fragments
of Pentecost restored
and lost before the tongue
has time for them. The word
is brought to nothing
that caught at burning bushes

gone already and at vistas
where there are none. For now
it must speak of the wreck
two rainbows make that
half-expunged, hang
one broken above the other
footlessly balancing.


## *Urlicht*

At the end of an unending war:
Horizons abide the deception
Of the sky's bright truce

But the dispersals have begun
There are no more roads
Only an immense dew

Of light
Over the dropped leafage
And in the room where

On the music-stand
The silent sonata lies
Open


## *Poem*

space
window
that looks into itself

a facing
both and
every way

colon
between green apple:
and vase of green

invisible
bed and breath
ebb and air-flow

below an unflawed
iridescence
of spiderweb


## Appearance

Snow brings into view the far hills:
    The winter sun feels for their surfaces:
Of the little we know of them, full half
    Is in the rushing out to greet them, the restraint
(Unfelt till then) melted at the look
    That gathers them in, to a meeting of expectations
With appearances. And what appears
    Where the slant-sided lit arena opens
Plane above plane, comes as neither
    Question nor reply, but a glance
Of fire, sizing our ignorance up,
    As the image seizes on us, and we grasp
For the ground that it delineates in a flight
    Of distances, suddenly stilled: the cold
Hills drawing us to a reciprocation,
    Ask words of us, answering images
To their range, their heights, held
    By the sun and the snow, between pause and change.


## Ars Poetica

*In memoriam A.A.*

What is it for
this form of saying, truce
with history in a language
no one may wish to use?

Who was it said
'a form of suicide'?—meaning
you drive yourself up to the edge
or as near as you can ride

without dropping over.
Some drop, wit-
less—and we
are to praise them for it?

Well, if mourning
were all we had,
we could settle for a great simplicity,
mourn ourselves mad.

But that is only half
the question: blight
has its cures and hopes
come uninvited.

What is it for? Answers
should be prepaid. And no Declines
of the West Full Stop
No selling lines.

# Mélisande

For Mélisande
flower-child of the forest
there were certain lacunae
in the short history of
her life: stoned
so many times
she could not recall
and she kept losing things
rings and things:
there was so little of her
she was mostly hair
and an impregnable innocence
gave an unthinking
rightness to whatever
she did or did not
do: the men she knew
slipped away
almost unnoticed
(she was not tenacious)
like rings and things:

—I had, she said
when she ended up
'beginning all over again'
and went home—I had
what you might call
a vision: and she needed one:
her mother
had forgotten to tell her
things and there was
nothing at all
half-way in her life such as
sorry or thankyou . . .
but they were together now
and in the evenings
mother sat
and read to her
*The Greening of America*
and other books like that
and so they lived
vapidly ever after


## Dialectic

*for Edoardo Sanguineti*

Life is the story of a body, you say:
the cough in the concert-hall is the story
of a body that cannot contain itself,
and the Waldstein the story of a life
refusing to be contained
by its body, the damaged ear
rebegetting its wholeness in posterities
of notes. I uncramp
bent knees. Side by side
all these itching legs! straining
to give back to the body
the rhythm out of the air and
heel-tap it into the ground.
A dropped programme tells
of a body lost to itself
and become all ear—ear
such as only the deaf
could dream of, with its gigantic

channels and circuits, its
snailshell of cartilage
brimming and quivering with the auricle's
passed-on story where
life is the breaking of silences
now heard, the daily remaking a body
refleshed of air.


## The Night-Train

composed
solely of carbon and soot-roses
freighted tight
with a million
minuscule statuettes
of La Notte (Night)
stumbles on
between unlit halts
till daylight begins
to bleed its jet
windows white, and the night-
train softly
discomposes, rose
on soot-rose,
to become—white
white white—
the snow-plough
that refuses to go.


## Event

Nothing is happening
Nothing

A waterdrop
Soundlessly shatters
A gossamer gives

Against this unused space
A bird
Might thoughtlessly try its voice
But no bird does

On the trodden ground
Footsteps
Are themselves more pulse than sound

At the return
A little drunk
On air

Aware that
Nothing
Is happening

# Comedy

It was when he began to see fields
As arguments, the ribbed ploughland
Contending with the direction of its fence:
If you went with the furrows, the view
From the fence disputed with you
Because you couldn't see it. If you sat still
The horizontals plainly said
You ought to be walking, and when you did
All you were leaving behind you proved
That you were missing the point. And the innumerable views
Kept troubling him, until
He granted them. Amen.

# Three Wagnerian Lyrics

## I. Liebestod

Tannhäuser wandered in the Venusberg:
 Spring's goddess had him for a season,
And no love living ever gave
 All that he knew there, and still craved
At his return. What could his lady
 Do but die?—She drew him after her
Deeper than ever spring could stir him.

## II. The Potion

King Mark who
Unwilling prognosticator
Of the *grand guignol viennois*
Despaired of ruling
His libidinal relatives,
Apologized
To them for them: 'The potion!
It was not your fault.'
Children of the times,
Absolved, they did not hear
The excuses he came to bring,
For one was dead and the other kept on singing.

## III. Good Friday

Easter and the resurrection
   Of the grass. Humbled Kundry
Dries the anointed feet of Parsifal
   With her hair. It is the imprisoned blood
Of Venus glows in the grail cup.

# Over Elizabeth Bridge: a Circumvention

To a friend in Budapest
'... my heart which owes this past a calm future.'
Attila József, *By the Danube*

Three years, now, the curve of Elizabeth Bridge
Has caught at some half-answering turn of mind—
Not recollection, but uncertainty
Why memory should need so long to find
A place and peace for it: that uncertainty
And restless counterpointing of a verse
'So wary of its I', Iván, is me:

Why should I hesitate to fix a meaning?
The facts were plain. A church, a riverside,
And, launched at the further bank, a parapet
Which, at its setting-out, must swerve or ride
Sheer down the bulk of the defenceless nave,
But with a curious sort of courteousness,
Bends by and on again. That movement gave

A pause to thoughts, which overeagerly
Had fed on fresh experience and the sense
That too much happened in too short a time
In this one city: self-enravelled, dense
With its own past, even its silence was
Rife with explanations, drummed insistent
As traffic at this church's window-glass.

How does the volley sound in that man's ears
Whom history did not swerve from, but elected
To face the squad? Was it indifference,
Fear, or sudden, helpless peace reflected
In the flash, for Imre Nagy?—another kind
Of silence, merely, that let in the dark
Which closed on Rajk's already silenced mind?

Here, past is half a ruin, half a dream—
Islanded patience, work of quiet hands,
Repainting spandrels that out-arched the Turk
In this interior. These are the lands
Europe and Asia, challenging to yield
A crop, or having raised one, harvest it,
Used for a highroad and a battlefield.

The bridge has paid the past its compliment:
The far bank's statuary stand beckoning
Where it flows, in one undeviating span,
Across the frozen river. That reckoning
Which József owed was cancelled in his blood,
And yet his promise veered beyond the act,
His verse grown calm with all it had withstood.[1]


## In Memoriam Thomas Hardy

How to speak with the dead
so that not only
our but their
words are valid?

[1] László Rajk, Hungarian Foreign Minister, executed during the Stalinist period; Imre
Nagy, Prime Minister and leader of the 1956 revolution, also executed. The poet, Attila
József, killed himself in the thirties.

Unlike their stones,
they scarcely resist us,
memory adjusting
its shades, its mist:

they are too like their photographs
where we can fill
with echoes of our regrets
· brown worlds of stillness.

His besetting word
was 'afterwards' and it released
their qualities, their restlessness
as though they heard it.


## Remembering Williams

'Wish we could talk today'
you wrote—no more
than that: the time before
it was: 'I stumbled
on a poem you had written', but the theme
lost itself, you forgot to say
what it was
'that called to mind
something over which
we had both been working, but had not
worked out by half.' Your wife
said she had done her mourning
while you still lived. Life
is a hard bed to lie on dying.


## The Apparition

I dreamed, Justine, we chanced on one another
    As though it were twenty years ago. Your dark
Too vulnerable beauty shone
    As then, translucent with its youth,
Unreal, as dreams so often are,
    With too much life. 'Tomorrow',

You said, 'we plough up the pastureland.'
    The clear and threatening sky
New England has in autumn—its heightened blue,
    The promise of early snow—were proofs enough
Of the necessity, though of what pastureland
    You spoke, I'd no idea. Then
Reading the meaning in your face, I found
    Your pastureland had been your hallowed ground which now
Must yield to use. And all of my refusals,
    All I feared, stood countered
By the resolve I saw in you and heard:
    While death itself, its certain thread
Twisted through the skein of consequence
    Seemed threatened by the strength
Of those dead years. It was a dream—
    No more; and you whom death
And solitude have tried, must know
    The treachery of dreams. And yet I do not think it lied,
Because it came, without insistence,
    Stood for a moment, spoke and then
Was gone, that apparition,
    Beyond the irresolute confines of the night,
Leaving me to weigh its words alone.


## Juliet's Garden

*J'ai connu une petite fille qui quittait son jardin
bruyamment, puis s'en revenait à pas de loup pour 'voir
comment il était quand elle n'était pas là'.*—Sartre

Silently . . .
she was quieter than breathing now,
hearing the garden seethe
behind her departed echo:

flowers merely grew,
showing no knowledge of her:
stones hunching their hardnesses
against her not being there:

scents came penetratingly,
rose, apple, and leaf-rot,
earthsmell under them all,
to where she was not:

such presences could only
rouse her fears,
ignoring and perfuming
this voluntary death of hers:

and so she came rushing back
into her garden then,
her new-found lack
the measure of all Eden.


## Against Portraits

How, beyond all foresight
or intention, light
plays with a face
whose features play with light:

frame on gilded frame,
ancestor on ancestor,
the gallery is filled
with more certainty than we can bear:

if there must be
an art of portraiture,
let it show us ourselves as we
break from the image of what we are:

the animation of speech, and then
the eyes eluding
that which, once spoken,
seems too specific, too concluding:

or, entering a sudden slant
of brightness, between dark and gold,
a face half-hesitant,
face at a threshold:

# Green Quinces

Ripening there
among the entanglement of leaves
that share their colour—
green quinces:
fragrantly free
from the contaminations
of daily envy,
the sight and suddenness
of green unknot
all that which thought
has ravelled where it cannot span
between the private and the public man—
between the motive
and the word:
the repeated and absurd
impulse to justify
oneself, knows
now its own
true colours:
it was the hardest-to-be-
put-down
vanity—desire
for the regard
of others. And how wrong
they were who taught us
green was the colour
should belong
to envy: they envied green.

# During Rain

Between
slats of the garden
bench, and strung
to their undersides
ride clinging
rain-drops, white
with transmitted
light as the bench
with paint: ranged

irregularly
seven staves of them
shine out
against the space
behind: untroubled
by the least breeze they
seem not to move
but one
by one as if
suddenly ripening
tug themselves free
and splash
down to be
replaced by an identical
and instant twin:
the longer you
look at it
the stillness proves
one flow unbroken
of new, false pearls,
dropped seeds of now
becoming then.


## Elegy for Henry Street

### for George and Mary Oppen

After the flight, the tired body
    Clung to the fading day of Henry Street:
There, it was hardly at an end, but midnight
    Weighed on the pulse of thought, its deep
Inconsistency working behind the eye
    That watched the lights come on—lights
Of the further shore, Manhattan's million
    Windows, floor on floor repeated
By the bay. I liked the street for its sordid
    Fiction of a small town order,
For its less and dingier glass
    As it let one down and back
Slowly out of transatlantic into human time,
    And its sooted bricks declared they were there
As they no longer are. 'Duck!' you cried, George,
    The day the militia filed out with rifles

At a Shriner celebration, but that was the pastoral era
　　Of sixty-six, and how should we or they
Have known, as taps were blowing, and the echoes,
　　Trapped in each scarred hallway
Meanly rhymed memory with civility,
　　They were bugling the burial of a place and time?


# Mistlines

Watching the mistlines flow slowly in
　　And fill the land's declivities that lay
Unseen until that indistinctness
　　Had acknowledged them, the eye
Grasps, at a glance, the mind's own
　　Food and substance, shape after shape
Emerging where all shapes drown;
　　For the mind is a hunter of forms:
Finding them wherever it may—in firm
　　Things or in frail, in vanishings—
It binds itself, in a world that must decay,
　　To present substance, and the words
Once said, present and substance
　　Both belie the saying. Mist
Drives on the house till forms become
　　The shapes of nearness, densities of home
Charged by their solitude—an island of
　　Daily objects mist has clarified
To the transparent calm in which you wear
　　The vestment of space that separates four walls,
Your flesh as certain and transitory as the world you share.


# Movements

## I.

I want that height and prospect such as music
　　Brings one to—music or memory,
When memory gains ground drowned-out
　　By years. I want the voyage of recovery,
The wind-torn eyrie and the mast-top
　　Sight of the horizon island,

Look-out tower compounded from pure sound:
    Trough on trough, valley after valley
Opens across the waves, between the dancing
    Leaves of the tree of time, and the broken chords
Space a footing for melody, borne-out above
    The haven of its still begetting, the hill
Of its sudden capture, not disembodied
    But an incarnation heard, a bird-flight
Shared, thrust and tendon and the answering air.


II.

The sky goes white. There is no bright alternation now
    Of lit cloud on blue: the scene's finality
Is robbed of a resonance. The day will end
    In its misting-over, its blending of muffled tones,
In a looking to nearnesses. A time
    Of colourlessness prepares for a recomposing,
As the prelude of quiet grows towards the true
    Prelude in the body of the hall. Anew we see
Nature as body and as building
    To be filled, if not with sound, then with
The thousand straying filamented ways
    We travel it by, from the inch before us to the height
Above, and back again. For travelling, we come
    To where we were; as if, in the rhymes
And repetitions and the flights of seeing,
    What we sought for was the unspoken
Familiar dialect of habitation—speech
    Behind speech, language that teaches itself
Under the touch and sight: a text
    That we must write, restore, complete
Grasping for more than the bare facts warranted
    By giving tongue to them. The sound
Of the thick rain chains us in liberty to where we are.


III.

Man, in an interior, sits down
    Before an audience of none, to improvise:
He is biding his time, for the rhymes
    That will arise at the threshold of his mind—
Pass-words into the castle-keep,
    The city of sleepers. Wakened by him,
Stanza by stanza (room by room)
    They will take him deeper in. Door

234

Opens on door, rhyme on rhyme,
  And the circling stair is always nearer
The further it goes. At last,
  He will hear by heart the music that he feared
Was lost, the crossing and the interlacing,
  The involutions of its tracery and the answering of part
By part, as the melody recedes, proceeds
  Above the beat, to twine, untwine
In search of a consonance between
  The pulse of the exploration and the pulse of line.

IV.

How soon, in the going down, will he
  Outdistance himself, lose touch to gain
The confidence of what would use him? Where
  Does he stand—beyond the customary ritual,
The habitual prayer? We live
  In an invisible church, a derisible hurt,
A look-out tower, point of powerlessness:
  The kingdom he has entered is a place
Of sources not of silences; memory does not rule it,
  But memory knows her own there
In finding names for them, reading
  By the flames the found words kindle
Their unburnable identities: the going down
  Is to a city of shapes, not a pit of shades
(For all ways begin, either from the eyes out
  Or the eyes in): to a Piazza del Campo
For spirits blessed by a consequence of days;
  For all that would speak itself aloud, a season
Of just regard, a light of sweetened reason.

V.

Man, in an exterior, sits down to say
  What it is he sees before him: to say
Is to see again by the light of speech
  Speechless, the red fox going
With intent, blind-eyed to all
  But prey. Human, our eyes
Stay with the green of an environment
  He only moves through, and man
In an exterior, tutelary spirit
  Of his own inheritance, speaks
To celebrate, entering on this action

235

That is a sort of acting, this assumption
Of a part where speech must follow
    As natural to the occasion, a doing which
Acts out the doer's being,
    Going beyond itself to clarify
The thing it is. But an actor
    May rehearse, sewing the speech behind his thoughts,
Readying them to come into his mind
    Before the words. Yet here, to think
Is say is see: and the red fox
    Caught where it patrols its cruel Eden,
Sets at a counter-pause
    The track of thought, as mounting the unsteady
Wall of crumbled ragstone, it halts its progress,
    A clear momentary silhouette, before it
Dips and disappears into wordlessness.

VI. *Written on water*

One returns to it, as though it were a thread
    Through the labyrinth of appearances, following-out
By eye, the stream in its unravelling,
    Deep in the mud-flanked gash the years
Have cut into scarpland: hard to read
    The life lines of erratic water
Where, at a confluence of two ways
    Refusing to be one without resistance,
Shoulderings of foam collide, unskein
    The moving calligraphy before
It joins again, climbing forward
    Across obstructions: but do you recall
That still pool—it also fed its stream—
    That we were led, night by night,
To return to, as though to clarify ourselves
    Against its depth, its silence? We lived
In a visible church, where everything
    Seemed to be at pause, yet nothing was:
The surface puckered and drew away
    Over the central depth; the foliage
Kept up its liquid friction
    Of small sounds, their multiplicity
A speech behind speech, continuing revelation
    Of itself, never to be revealed:
It rendered new (time within time)
    An unending present, travelling through

All that we were to see and know:
  'Written on water', one might say
Of each day's flux and lapse,
  But to speak of water is to entertain the image
Of its seamless momentum once again,
  To hear in its wash and grip on stone
A music of constancy behind
  The wide promiscuity of acquaintanceship,
Links of water chiming on one another,
  Water-ways permeating the rock of time.

## Curtain Call

The dead in their dressing rooms
sweat out the sequel
through greasepaint and brocade
O to have died
on the last note of a motif, flangeing home
the dovetails of sweet necessity . . . But the applause
draws them on to resurrection.
No one has won.
Time has undone the incurables
by curing them. The searoar of hands
throbbing, ebbing, each castaway
starts to explore his island. Vans
are standing outside now,
ready for palaces and caverns where
past hoardings and houses
boarded against demolition
a late-night traffic
turning its headlamps towards the peripheries gives
caller and called
back to their own unplotted lives.

# THE WAY IN
# AND OTHER POEMS
### (1974)

# The Way In

The needle-point's swaying reminder
   Teeters at thirty, and the flexed foot
Keeps it there. Kerb-side signs
   For demolitions and new detours,
A propped pub, a corner lopped, all
   Bridle the pressures that guide the needle.

I thought I knew this place, this face
   A little worn, a little homely.
But the look that shadows softened
   And the light could grace, keeps flowing away from me
In daily change; its features, rendered down,
   Collapse expressionless, and the entire town

Sways in the fume of the pyre. Even the new
   And mannerless high risers tilt and wobble
Behind the deformations of acrid heat—
   A century's lath and rafters. Bulldozers
Gobble a street up, but already a future seethes
   As if it had waited in the crevices:

A race in transit, a nomad hierarchy:
   Cargoes of debris out of these ruins fill
Their buckled prams: their trucks and hand-carts wait
   To claim the dismantlings of a neighbourhood—
All that a grimy care from wastage gleans,
   From scrap-iron down to heaps of magazines.

Slowing, I see the faces of a pair
   Behind their load: he shoves and she
Trails after him, a sexagenarian Eve,
   Their punishment to number every hair
Of what remains. Their clothes come of their trade—
   They wear the cast-offs of a lost decade.

The place had failed them anyhow, and their pale
   Absorption staring past this time
And dusty space we occupy together,
   Gazes the new blocks down—not built for them;
But what they are looking at they do not see.
   No Eve, but mindless Mnemosyne,

She is our lady of the nameless metals, of things
  No hand has made, and no machine
Has cut to a nicety that takes the mark
  Of clean intention—at best, the guardian
Of all that our daily contact stales and fades,
  Rusty cages and lampless lampshades.

Perhaps those who have climbed into their towers
  Will eye it all differently, the city spread
In unforeseen configurations, and living with this,
  Will find that civility I can only miss—and yet
It will need more than talk and trees
  To coax a style from these disparities.

The needle-point's swaying reminder
  Teeters: I go with uncongealing traffic now
Out onto the cantilevered road, window on window
  Sucked backwards at the level of my wheels.
Is it patience or anger most renders the will keen?
  This is a daily discontent. This is the way in.


# Night Ride

The lamps are on: terrestrial galaxies,
  Fixed stars and moving. How many lights,
How many lives there are, cramped in beside
  This swathe of roadway. And its sodium circuits
Have ousted the glimmer of a thousand hearths
  To the margins of estates whose windows
Blaze over pastoral parentheses. Scatterings
  Trace out the contours of heights unseen,
Drip pendants across their slopes.
  Too many of us are edging behind each other
With dipped beams down the shining wet.
  Our lights seem more beautiful than our lives
In the pulse and grip of this city with neither
  Time nor space in which to define
Itself, its style, as each one feels
  His way among the catseyes and glittering asterisks
And home on home reverberates our wheels.

# At Stoke

I have lived in a single landscape. Every tone
  And turn have had for their ground
These beginnings in grey-black: a land
  Too handled to be primary—all the same,
The first in feeling. I thought it once
  Too desolate, diminished and too tame
To be the foundation for anything. It straggles
  A haggard valley and lets through
Discouraged greennesses, lights from a pond or two.
  By ash-tips, or where the streets give out
In cindery in-betweens, the hills
  Swell up and free of it to where, behind
The whole vapoury, patched battlefield,
  The cows stand steaming in an acrid wind.
This place, the first to seize on my heart and eye,
  Has been their hornbook and their history.


# Hokusai on the Trent

This milky sky of a dragging afternoon
  Seems a painter's sky—the vision of a lack,
A thwarted possibility that broods
  On the meanness and exclusion. This could well be
An afternoon sunk in eternity
  But for the traffic tolling the rush hour
Among blackened houses, back to back
  And the tang of the air (its milk is sour):
And what painting could taste of such dragging afternoons
  Whose tints are tainted, whose Fujiyamas slag?


# Etruria Vale

  Nineteen-thirty, our window had for view
  The biggest gasometer in England.
  Time, no doubt, has robbed that record, too.
  The waste ground disappeared beneath the houses.
  Faced with the scale of all this, I'm as lost
  As if I were Josiah Wedgwood's ghost

Compelled to follow out the tow-path through
The place he named Etruria. In the darkness
He might still bark his shins against the rungs
His barges moored beside. His sooted house
Flares nightly in the gusty lightnings as
The foundries pour their steel. The plan had been
A factory and model cottages,
A seat and prospect for a gentleman,
But history blackened round him, time drank up
The clear wine of his intention, left the lees
Staining the bottom of the valley's cup.
The gas tank has the air of an antique.
And nineteen-thirty was another century.


## Gladstone Street

It was the place to go in nineteen-thirty,
And so we went. A housemaid or two
Still lingered on at the bigger houses.
A miner and his family were the next
To follow us there, had scarcely settled in
When the wife began dying, whitely visible
Through the bay window in their double bed.
At the back, the garden vanished
Under grass and a ramshackle shed.
People were sure the street was going downhill.
It literally was: cracks in our hall
Opened as the house started to subside
Towards the mines beneath. Miners were everywhere
Under that cancerous hill. My mother swore
That you could hear them tapping away below
Of a quiet night. Miners unnerved her so
Ever since one sat beside her on the train
And soiled her with his pit dirt. But it wasn't miners
Undid the street. The housemaids lasted
Until the war, then fed the factories.
Flat-dwellers came and went, in the divided houses,
Mothers unwedded who couldn't pay their rent.
A race of gardeners died, and a generation
Hacked down the walls to park their cars
Where the flowers once were. It was there it showed,
The feeble-minded style of the neighbourhood

Gone gaudily mad in painted corrugations,
Botches of sad carpentry. The street front has scarcely changed.
No one has recorded the place.
Perhaps we shall become sociology. We have outpaced
Gladstone's century. We might have been novels.

## Dates: Penkhull New Road

It was new about eighteen-sixty.
Eighteen-sixty had come to stay, and did
Until the war—the second war, I mean.
Wasn't forty-five our nineteen-seventeen—
The revolution we had all of us earned?
Streamers and trestles in the roadway:
Even the climate rhymed with the occasion
And no drop fell. Eighteen-sixty
The architecture still insisted, gravely neat:
Alleyways between the houses, doors
That opened onto a still car-less street.
Doorsteps were once a civil place. There must have been a date
It came to be thought common and too late
In time, to be standing shouting out there
Across to the other side—the side
I envied, because its back-yards ran sheer
To the factory wall, warm, black, pulsating,
A long, comforting brick beast. I returned
In seventy-three. Like England,
The place had half-moved with the times—the 'other side'
Was gone. Something had bitten a gap
Out of the stretch we lived in. Penkhull still crowned
The hill, rebuilt to a plan—may as well scrap
The architectural calendar: that dream
Was dreamed up by the insurance-man
And we've a long time to live it yet.
The factory wore a half-bereaved, half-naked look . . .
It took time to convince me that I cared
For more than beauty: I write to rescue
What is no longer there—absurd
A place should be more fragile than a book.

# Portrait of the Artist I

One day, his mother took him on the tram.
An octogenarian in a mackintosh
Who still possessed the faculty for veneration,
Leaned across the aisle to her and said:
'That boy of yours has a remarkable forehead—
He'll live to be lord mayor.' He didn't rise
To that, but forehead letting instinct choose,
Betrayed him into verse. So Whittington
Never turned again, his mother strayed
Bemused between the prophecy and its failure.
The tram-lines were dragged up the very next year.

# Portrait of the Artist II

Season of mists and migraines, rich catarrhs,
Pipes in the public library throbbed and hissed
Against your advent. Parks were emptying.
Soaked benches and a wind that brought the grime
Smoking across the beds, now flowerless,
Drove old men indoors to the reading room.
They took their time, pored over magazines
They scarcely saw, and breathed-in dust and newsprint,
Clearing their throats to splatter on the floor.
Across the street, the high school lunch-hour raged.
He brought his sandwiches inside. Of course,
It was forbidden. The old illiterates, too,
Dragged orts and fragments from their paper bags.
A schoolboy and a dozen ancients, they
Watched for the librarian's bureaucracy
Who tried to spy them out, but seldom could—
They'd grown so adept at their secret feeding,
Bent at those tables others used for reading . . .
Did the old guilt stick? For now, he wrote
His verses furtively, on blotters, minutes,
As though back there, that surreptitious snack
Still hidden by *The Illustrated London News*.

# The Tree

This child, shovelling away
what remains of snow—
a batter of ash and crystals—
knows nothing of the pattern
his bent back lifts
above his own reflection:
it climbs the street-lamp's stem
and cross-bar, branching
to take in all the lines
from gutter, gable, slates
and chimney-crowns to the high
pillar of a mill chimney
on a colourless damp sky:
there in its topmost air
and eyrie rears that tree
his bending sends up
from a treeless street, its roots
in the eye and in the net the shining
flagstones spread at his feet.


# Midlands

Rain baptizes the ravaged counties
    In the name of some god who can remember
The way the land lay, the groundswell
    Under it all. The football club,
Treading back to mud their threadbare pitch,
    Move garish on the grey, hemmed-
In by a throng of sodden houses
    Whose Sunday kitchens grow savoury for them.


# In the Ward

Old women come here to die. Nurses
    Tend them with a sort of callous zest
That keeps their youthful patience, guarantees it
    In face of all they do not wish to be:
Shrunk limbs, shrunk lives, the incontinence.

A woodland scene is hanging on the wall,
To rectify some lost connection
　　With a universe that goes on shepherding its flock
Of fogs out there, its unkillable seasons.
　　Dying, these old have for an ally still
That world of repetitions for, once gone,
　　They are replaced incessantly. In the ward
The picture-glass gives back the outlines
　　Of both old and young, in a painted
Sunlight and among the twines of trees.


# The Marl Pits

It was a language of water, light and air
　　I sought—to speak myself free of a world
Whose stoic lethargy seemed the one reply
　　To horizons and to streets that blocked them back
In a monotone fume, a bloom of grey.
　　I found my speech. The years return me
To tell of all that seasoned and imprisoned:
　　I breathe familiar, sedimented air
From a landscape of disembowellings, underworlds
　　Unearthed among the clay. Digging
The marl, they dug a second nature
　　And water, seeping up to fill their pits,
Sheeted them to lakes that wink and shine
　　Between tips and steeples, streets and waste
In slow reclaimings, shimmers, balancings,
　　As if kindling Eden rescinded its own loss
And words and water came of the same source.


# Class

Those midland *a*'s
once cost me a job:
diction defeated my best efforts—
I was secretary at the time
to the author of *The Craft of Fiction*.
That title was full of class.
You had only to open your mouth on it
to show where you were born

and where you belonged. I tried
time and again I tried
but I couldn't make it
that top *A—ah*
I should say—
it sounded like gargling.
I too visibly shredded his fineness:
it was clear the job couldn't last
and it didn't. Still, I'd always thought him an ass
which he pronounced arse. There's no accounting for taste.

## *The Rich*

I like the rich—the way
they say: 'I'm not made of money':
their favourite pastoral
is to think they're not rich at all—
poorer, perhaps, than you or me,
for they have the imagination of that fall
into the pinched decency
we take for granted. Of course,
they do want to be wanted
by all the skivvies and scrapers
who neither inherited nor rose.
But are they daft or deft,
when they proclaim themselves
men of the left, as if prepared
at the first premonitory flush
of the red dawn
to go rushing onto the street
and, share by share,
add to the common conflagration
their scorned advantage?
They know that it can't happen
in Worthing or Wantage:
with so many safety valves
between themselves and scalding,
all they have to fear
is wives, children, breath and balding.
And at worst
there is always some sunny
Aegean prospect. I like the rich—
they so resemble the rest
of us, except for their money.

# Bridges

The arteries, red lane on lane,
    Cover the engineers' new maps:
England lies lost to silence now:
    On bridges, where old roads cross
The chasm of the new, the idlers
    Stand staring down. Philosophers
Of the common run, some masticate pipe-stems,
    And seem not to hear the roar in Albion's veins,
As though the quiet, rebegotten as they lean, survived
    Through them alone, its stewards and sustainers,
For all these advancing and disappearing lives.

# At Saint Mary's Church

The high nave, in a place of ships,
    Seems like the invitation to some voyage
Long deferred. It will not be undertaken now.
    Saint Mary's shares a horizon
With blocks in a mock stone-brown
    Meant to resemble hers. This cheek by jowl affair
Labours to prove we can equal or outdo
    Those eras of cholera, fear of the mob.
If that is true, it is not true here.
    Elizabeth thought this church the comeliest
She had seen, and haunts it still, solid
    In painted wood, and carved by the same
Hands as those, that in a place of ships,
    Shaped gaudy figure-heads. And though
That voyage is not to be undertaken, she,
    All bright will, female insouciance,
Might well have been the thrust and prow
    To such a venture now forsaken
In the dust of abolished streets, the land-
    Locked angles of a stale geometry.

                                 *Bristol*

# In a Brooklyn Park

'To people these lands with civil men',
   George Jackson said. There is civility enough
Inside this place, if one could spread it:
   A woman is trying to reconcile
Two fighting boys who still refuse
   To smile with the bright persuasion of her smile;
An old man sits learning from a book
   *Inglés sin Maestro*, while among the trees
Wander three generations of the Jews.


# Under the Moon's Reign

Twilight was a going of the gods: the air
   Hung weightlessly now—its own
Inviolable sign. From habit, we
   Were looking still for what we could not see—
The inside of the outside, for some spirit flung
   From the burning of that Götterdämmerung
And suffused in the obscurity. Scraps
   Of the bare-twigged scene were floating
Scattered across scraps of water—mirrors
   Shivered and stuck into a landscape
That drifted visibly to darkness. The pools
   Restrained the disappearing shapes, as all around
The dusk was gaining: too many images
   Beckoned from that thronging shade
None of which belonged there. And then the moon
   Drawing all into more than daylight height
Had taken the zenith, the summit branches
   Caught as by steady lightning, and each sign
Transformed, but by no more miracle than the place
   It occupied and the eye that saw it
Gathered into the momentary perfection of the scene
   Under transfigured heavens, under the moon's reign.

# Foxes' Moon

Night over England's interrupted pastoral,
  And moonlight on the frigid lattices
Of pylons. The shapes of dusk
  Take on an edge, refined
By a drying wind and foxes bring
  Flint hearts and sharpened senses to
This desolation of grisaille in which the dew
  Grows clearer, colder. Foxes go
In their ravenous quiet to where
  The last farm meets the first
Row from the approaching town: they nose
  The garbage of the yards, move through
The white displacement of a daily view
  Uninterrupted. Warm sleepers turn,
Catch the thin volpine bark between
  Dream on dream, then lose it
To the babbling undertow they swim. These
  Are the fox hours, cleansed
Of all the meanings we can use
  And so refuse them. Foxes glow,
Ghosts unacknowledged in the moonlight
  Of the suburb, and like ghosts they flow
Back, racing the coming red, the beams
  Of early cars, a world not theirs
Gleaming from kindled windows, asphalt, wires.

# The Dream

Under that benign calm eye that sees
  Nothing of the vista of land and sky
It brings to light; under the interminably
  Branching night, of street and city,
Vein and artery, a dream
  Held down his mind that blinded him
To all except the glimmering, closed-in warmth
  Of his own present being. Alone
And yet aware within that loneliness
  Of what he shared with others—a sense
Of scope and pleasure in mere warmth—
  He seemed the measure of some constricted hope

That asked a place in which it might pursue
  Its fulness, and so grew away from him,
Swayed into palpability like a wall:
  He knew that he must follow out its confine
To his freedom, and be taught this tense fluidity
  Always a thought beyond him. His hand
Still feeling for that flank of stone,
  The space that opened round him might have grown there
For the resurrection of a being buried
  By the reality that too much defined it: now
The transitions of the dream, the steps and streets,
  The passageways that branched beneath
Haphazard accumulation of moon on moon,
  Spurned at each turn a reality
Merely given—an inert threat
  To be met with and accommodated. The ways
He walked seemed variants on a theme
  Shaped by a need that was greed no longer,
The dream of a city under the city's dream,
  Proportioned to the man whom sleep replenishes
To stand reading with opened eyes
  The intricacies of the imagined spaces there
Strange and familiar as the lines that map a hand.


# *After a Death*

A little ash, a painted rose, a name.
  A moonshell that the blinding sky
Puts out with winter blue, hangs
  Fragile at the edge of visibility. That space
Drawing the eye up to its sudden frontier
  Asks for a sense to read the whole
Reverted side of things. I wanted
  That height and prospect such as music brings—
Music or memory. Neither brought me here.
  This burial place straddles a green hill,
Chimneys and steeples plot the distances
  Spread vague below: only the sky
In its upper reaches keeps
  An untarnished January colour. Verse
Fronting that blaze, that blade,
  Turns to retrace the path of its dissatisfactions,

Thought coiled on thought, and only certain that
    Whatever can make bearable or bridge
The waste of air, a poem cannot.
    The husk of moon, risking the whole of space,
Seemingly sails it, fraily launched
    To its own death and fulness. We buried
A little ash. Time so broke you down,
    Your lost eyes, dry beneath
Their matted lashes, a painted rose
    Seems both to memorialize and mock
What you became. It picks your name out
    Written on the roll beside a verse—
Obstinate words: measured against the blue,
    They cannot conjure with the dead. Words,
Bringing that space to bear, that air
    Into each syllable we speak, bringing
An earnest to us of the portion
    We must inherit, what thought of that would give
The greater share of comfort, greater fear—
    To live forever, or to cease to live?
The imageless unnaming upper blue
    Defines a world, all images
Of endeavours uncompleted. Torn levels
    Of the land drop, street by street,
Pitted and pooled, its wounds
    Cleansed by a light, dealt out
With such impartiality you'd call it kindness,
    Blindly assuaging where assuagement goes unfelt.


## Elemental

A last flame,
sole leaf
flagging at the tree tip,
is dragged through the current
down into the water
of the air, and in this final
metamorphosis, spiralling
swims to earth.

# In December

Cattle are crowding the salt-lick.
The gruel of mud icily thickens.
On the farm-boy's Honda a sweat of fog drops.
They are logging the woodland, the sole standing crop.

# Hyphens

'The country's love-
liness', it said:
what I read was
'the country's love-
lines'—the unnec-
essary 's'
passed over by
the mind's blind-
ly discriminating eye:
but what I saw
was a whole scene
restored: the love-
lines drawing
together the list
'loveliness' capped
and yet left
vague, unloved:
lawns, gardens, houses,
the encircling trees.

# In March

These dry, bright winter days,
    When the crow's colour takes to itself
Such gloss, the shadows from the hedge
    Ink-stain half way across
The road to where a jagged blade
    Of light eats into them: light's guarded frontier
Is glittering everywhere, everywhere held
    Back by naked branchwork, dark
Fissurings along the creviced walls,

Shade side of barn and house, of half-cut stack
Strawing the ground, in its own despite
    With flecks of pallid gold, allies to light:
And over it all, a chord of glowing black
    A shining, flying shadow, the crow is climbing.


# Discrepancies

That year, March began in April.
Wasn't it floes from Greenland
Going south, they said, and the earthquake
In Nicaragua—a collision between
The seismic and the atmospheric that released
An effervescence into the air? Its tang and sting
Excited the nostrils of the yearling,
The dead leaves circling rose again
But the clouds said, 'Snow, snow',
The sun melting the threat before it fell.
Nicaragua blazed into the chaos,
A polar glittering of gulls
Swung round and round on the mid-air currents
Over the windswept bed of their inland sea.
Nature has evolved beyond us—
You couldn't have painted it, I mean,
Unless on the whirlpool's fish-eye mirror
Where the blinding navel winds all discrepancies in.


# The Last of Night

Mist after frost. The woodlands
stretch vague in it, but catch
the rising light on reefs
of foliage above the greyish
'sea' I was about to say,
but sun so rapidly advances
between glance and word,
under that leafy headland
mist lies a sea no more:
a gauze visibly fading
burns out to nothing, lets grow

beneath each mid-field bush
a perfect shadow, and among
frost-whitened tussocks
the last of night recedes along
tracks the animals have taken
back into earth and wood.


## The Witnesses

Now that the hillside woods are dense with summer,
    One enters with a new, an untaught sense
Of heights and distances. Before,
    Lacking the profusion, the protrusion of the leaves,
Spaces seemed far shallower that, now,
    Thronged with ledges of overhanging green,
Bear down on the air beneath. One can no longer see
    The high recession stretching beyond each tree,
But the view, shut round, lets through
    The mind into a palpitation of jostled surfaces.
Nudging, they overlap, reach out
    Beckoning, bridging the underdeeps that stir
Unsounded among the foliage of a hundred trees
    That fill an aerial city's every thoroughfare
With the steady vociferation of unhuman witnesses.


## Hill Walk

*for Philippe and Anne-Marie Jaccottet*

Innumerable and unnameable, foreign flowers
    Of a reluctant April climbed the slopes
Beside us. Among them, rosemary and thyme
    Assuaged the coldness of the air, their fragrance
So intense, it seemed as if the thought
    Of that day's rarity had sharpened sense, as now
It sharpens memory. And yet such pungencies
    Are there an affair of every day—Provençal
Commonplaces, like the walls, recalling
    In their broken sinuousness, our own
Limestone barriers, half undone
    By time, and patched against its sure effacement

257

To retain the lineaments of a place.
   In our walk, time used us well that rhymed
With its own herbs. We crested idly
   That hill of ilexes and savours to emerge
Along the plateau at last whose granite
   Gave on to air: it showed us then
The place we had started from and the day
   Half gone, measured against the distances
That lay beneath, a territory travelled.
   All stretched to the first fold
Of that unending landscape where we trace
   Through circuits, drops and terraces
The outworks, ruinous and overgrown,
   Where space on space has labyrinthed past time:
The unseizable citadel glimmering back at us,
   We contemplated no assault, no easy victory:
Fragility seemed sufficiency that day
   Where we sat by the abyss, and saw each hill
Crowned with its habitations and its crumbled stronghold
   In the scents of inconstant April, in its cold.

## *Lacoste*

De Sade's rent walls let in
   Through faceless windows, a sky
As colourless as the stones that framed them:
   All tenacity, a dry ivy grew
Bristling against the grey. But wild thyme
   Sweetened anew the memory of the spot,
Its scent as fresh as a single fig-tree's
   Piercing greenness. The only words
I heard in that place were kind ones—
   'If you would care to visit my house . . .'
—And came from the old woman who
   Paused in climbing the broken street
At meeting us: but we were *en voyage*
   So she, wishing us a good one, bent on
Once more against the devious, sloped track,
   We winding down a descent that led
Back to the valley vineyards' spread geometry.

# How Far

How far from us
even the nearest are
among these close leaves
crowding the window:

what we know
of that slow then sudden
bursting into green is merely
what we have seen of it and not

(fermenting at its heart)
darkness such as the blind might hear:
for us, there is no way in where
across these surfaces

the light is a white lie
told only to hide the dark
extent from us
of a seafloor continent.


# Tiger Skull

Frozen in a grimace, all cavernous threat,
onslaught remains its sole end still:
handle it, and you are taught the weight
such a thrust to kill would carry.

The mind too eagerly marries a half truth. This carapace
lies emptied of the memory of its own sated peace,
its bestial repose and untensed pride
under the equanimity of sun and leaf,

where to be tiger is
to move through the uncertain terrain supple-paced:
how little this stark and armoured mouth can say
of the living beast.

# The Greeting

One instant of morning
he cast a glance
idly, half blindly
into the depths of distance:

space and its Eden
of green and blue
warranted more watching
than such gazing through:

but the far roofs gave
a 'Good day' back,
defeating that negligence
with an unlooked-for greeting:

it was the day's one time
that the light on them
would carry their image
as far as to him

then abandon the row,
its lit-up walls
and unequal pitches,
its sharpness to shadow:

one instant of morning
rendered him time
and opened him space,
one whole without seam.


# The Insistence of Things

*paragraphs from a journal*

At the edge of conversations, uncompleting all acts of thought, looms the insistence of things which, waiting on our recognition, face us with our own death, for they are so completely what we are not. And thus we go on trying to read them, as if they were signs, or the embodied message of oracles. We remember how Orpheus drew voices from the stones.

It takes so long to become aware of the places we inhabit. Not so much of the historic or geographic facts attaching to them, as of the moment to moment quality of a given room, or of the simple recognitions that could be lured to inhabit a paragraph, a phrase, a snatch of words—and thus speak to us.

A stump of stone juts up out of the grass, glittering drily like weathered cedar. A cloud of gnats dances over it on a now mild December day. It is the remains of a mounting block, disused beside this fenced-off bridge. The gnats haunt the stone as if it held warmth, grey against grey. One can scarcely make out what they are, and their winter dance seems such a weightless celebration of improbables (how did they escape last night's frost?—the birds of the day before?) that what one actually sees is more than the sight—an instance radiating unlooked-for instances, a swarm of unreasoning hopes suddenly and vulnerably brought into the open.

Snow keeps trying the currents of the air—a haze, a smoke of crystals—but each time it is about to take solid shape, the wind whirls it apart into specks of white dust, just visible on the blackness of the surrounding woodland. The thin cry of an early lamb is brought in on the blustering wind that crashes endlessly against the trees. There is an almost metallic edge to that frail voice with which a new energy has entered among the leafless branches, the sudden sun-gashes in dark cloud and lancings of green over shallow grass where the rays emerge.

Beech leaves on a small beech, crowded and protected by the closeness of an ill-kept wood. For all the storms, they are still firmly anchored and look like brittle, even fragments of brown paper, their veining very clear and regular. The wind in them hisses faintly, a distinct and crisper hiss than that of the water which fills the distances. The coming and going breaths of the wind: hiss, silence, hiss. The pale brown of the leaves seems among the dark branches to attract light into these scalloped and cupped handshapes.

Towards the end of a warm spring day, the evening air, echoing with bird-calls, prepares for frost. A distant half moon in its halo. No cloud near it, only down low on the western horizon where it lies shapeless, thick and pink-purple, more like a mist. In the east, a few feathery drifters also catching the pink, last flare. The map on the moon is visible. A sound as clearly isolated as the moon (a shut door) breaks off from the farm building. The thin cry of lambs, a discussion of rooks above the wood, the insistence of bird-calls. The sound of a farm van winds away through the mingled callings. The rooks are flying round and round in the twilight over the wood, like dirty sediment rising and falling in the water of the air. They argue (or agree?—which?) on one concerted note.

A sudden intervention from two wild ducks. An owl takes up the broken note of the ducks, rounds it, mellows it, hollows it to a scream, hoarsely answering a second owl in a new dialogue. As the daylight disappears, the moon casts pallid shadows.

## Idrigill

Roofless, the wreck of a house and byre
    Lies like a stone boat, the tide
Behind, inching, ebbing. A high
    Sea could almost float it out
Across that plain of water, to where
    Those who abandoned it still try
To account for their lives here
    Levelled too long, too soon:
Working the waves, they gather up salt sheaves
    That, collapsing, break their hold and spread
In abysses of candour, scatterings of fools' gold.
    That boat would take them in,
Beach them by sea-caves where they might lie
    And face out the storms in sea-cleansed effigy,
If grass had not matted its decks and clasped them down
    To a tranquil earth its owners could never own.

## Of Lady Grange

Of Lady Grange
    that ill-starred daughter
    of Chiesly of Dalry: he
    who when the Lord President
    sat in adverse judgement
    murdered him:

She inherited
    the violence of her father, was married
    some say against her will, others
    so that she might spy on him
    to Erskine, my Lord Grange,
    Jacobite, profligate and bigot:

He
        and the family she bore him
        detested her: but when a separation
        was arranged, my Lady Grange went on
        molesting him, opposed as she was
        to his politics and his person:

One night—
        it was a decade and more
        after the rebellion and its failure—
        her husband and his friends
        gathered, each to rehearse his part
        in the restoration of the house of Stuart:

The lives
        of men of great family
        were at stake when she, concealed
        it is said beneath a sofa
        or a day-bed where they sat,
        burst forth and threatened to betray them:

James Erskine
        judging her capable of that,
        two gentlemen (attended)
        called at her lodging: her resistance
        cost her two teeth as they forced her
        first into a sedan, then on to horse:

Her husband
        had it given out that she
        was sick of a fever: the next day
        she 'died' of it and he
        saw to it that her funeral should
        have all of the ceremony due to blood:

Her journey
        was as cold as the earth
        her coffin lay in:
        air, spray and the spread of water
        awaited the living woman
        her stone mocked greyly:

They rode
    from Edinburgh to Stirling and despite
    storms, robbers, Highland
    tracks and the lack of them,
    reached the deserted Castle Tirrim
    at Moidart loch:

Thence
    on by boat, and out
    into the Atlantic: Heiskir
    was to house her two years,
    until the single family there
    could no longer tolerate her

And said so:
    from a ship, two men
    appeared and carried her
    on board to Kilda, where
    no one could speak her language,
    nor would she learn theirs:

She learned
    to spin and in a clew
    of yarn sent with her neighbours' wool
    to Inverness, she hid a message,
    though she had neither pen nor pencil:
    this was the sixth year of her exile:

To Hope,
    her misnamed lawyer,
    the letter seemed
    to be written in blood: a ship
    chartered, fitted and sent
    found without its tenant

The house
    on Kilda, chimneyless, earth-floored:
    for her, once more
    the inevitable sea, Skye
    at last and the sand of a sea-cave
    where fish-nets hung to dry

At Idrigill:
      nor could this place
      keep the secret long:
      though the cliffs hung sheer,
      the fishers came
      to cure their catch and to sleep here:

Again
      she must be moved on
      and over to Uist: a large
      boulder, knotted in a noose,
      lay in the boat: a guard stood
      ready to sink his charge

If
      rounding a headland of the cliff
      the ship, sighting them,
      should pursue: out into the surge
      oars drew them where
      the three wrecked women

Emerge
      from the sea in stone:
      they were set for the further isles:
      Bracadale sank down
      behind them into its mist:
      now they could only trust

Time
      to weary what vigilance
      might try, and time
      so ruffled and so smoothed
      the sea-lanes they went by,
      was it from Uist, Harris or Assynt

That she
      came back to Skye?
      Of the life she had
      in Vaternish, all we hear
      is of the madness of her last
      and fifteenth year

In exile,
      of 'the poor, strange lady
      who came ashore
      and died', and of the great
      funeral which the Macleod
      of Ramsay's portrait, paid for:

Yet still
      no ordinary end
      attended that lonely woman:
      'for reasons unknown'
      the coffin at Duirinish
      held stones only:

But there
      where Kilconan church
      still points at variable skies
      a roofless gable, the square
      stone of a later year
      confesses her corpse:

She
      is well buried above that sea,
      the older dead beside her
      murdered in the burning church
      and, below, their slayers on the same
      day slain, the dyke-wall toppled to cover them.


## The Promise

The tide goes down, uncovering its gifts:
    Rocks glint with the silver of slivered wood,
Like the piecemeal skeleton of some great boat,
    That this light of resurrection, if it could
Would draw together again, and the next tide find
    As solid as the cliff that looms behind
Its absence now. But part of a scene
    That is flawed and flowing, the pieces lie
Under a fragmented rainbow's promise
    Of the changes in their unbroken sufficiency.

## Marine

The water, wind-impelled, advancing
    Along the promontory side, continually
Shaves off into spray, where its flank
    Grazes against rock, each white
In-coming rush like a vast
    Wheel spun to nothing, a wing
Caught down from flight to feathers.


## Rubh An' Dunain

### (The Point of the Forts)

Mouthings of water at the end of a world.
Pictish masons have outreached their enemy
In stone. But who won, or what gods
Saved the bare appearances of it all
Is written in no history.
Their pantheon was less powerful than this wall.


## Couplet

Light catches the sudden metal of the streams:
Their granite captive is stirring in its chains.


## Beethoven Attends the C Minor Seminar

That was the day they invited
Ludmilla Quatsch, the queen of the sleevenote.
Her works cannot be quoted
Without permission. I shall not quote.

Think and drink were to be paid for
Out of the Gabbocca Fund.
Her theme was 'Arguing About Music'. Her arguments
Had driven T. Melvin Quatsch into the ground.

She challenged Beethoven on the Heiliger Dankgesang:
Too long. Too long. She argued
For a C Minor without final chords
And a Hymn to Joy without the words.

Ah, if only he were here in spirit to agree!
(She knew that she had him confuted)
And suddenly, inexplicably there he was—
Some confusion of levels in the celestial computer

Had earthed him. It was the briefest of appearances,
But up out of vagueness wavering
He seemed to savour her points, and she
Clutched for his attention, all cadenzas and fortissimi.

She had sensed at once the urgency of the event,
Packed-in and pressure-cooked her argument:
By now, the laity were quite lost
As she pitched her apophthegms at that height, that ghost.

He seemed to grow very deaf, and then
(After a slight cybernetic adjustment overhead)
Very dead and disappeared.
Had all she was saying gone unheard?

She thought she still could descry him—
He of the impregnable ear, still quick
To catch only the most hidden sound:
His silence was as unanswerable as his music.

Doubt diminished her. They helped her out.
After which those sleevenotes were never the same
(Too complicated, as I have said, to quote)
—Rumour insisted it was another hand from which they came.

When they invited Ludmilla, all had hoped
That she might return to fill the chair,
But that untimely vision balked
Them and her of twenty years of talk.

# Consolations for Double Bass

You lament your lot at the bottom of an abyss
   Of moonlight. And yet you would not
Change it for all that bland redundance
   Overhead, the great theme leaping
Chromatic steeps in savage ease.
   The trumpets on their fugal stair
Climb each other's summits pair by pair:
   A memorial of remissive drums. The hero falls.
A race of disappointed generals, we mourn him
   *Nobilmente*. Confluence of a hundred streams
In one lambency of sound, our grief
   Beckons the full orchestra, 'Come on—
Crash in like a house collapsing
   On top of its hardware.' And you?
All that you can do is state, repeat,
   For repetition is the condition for remembering
What must come—the moment
   For the return to earth, to blood-beat.
Good gut, resonant belly,
   You are the foot a hundred others
Tread by, the bound of their flying islands
   And their utopias of sound. Tristan is being sung to
Like a drowsy suckling: you
   Are sanchoing still: that, I know,
Is the story of another hero—but you have ridden
   With them all to their distress, and lived
To punctuate it, unastounded in your endless
   Unthanked *Hundesleben*, nose to ground.


# *Melody*

*Song is being . . .* RILKE

That phrase in the head—that snatch repeated
   Could have led nowhere, but for the will
To hear the consequence of it—the reply
   To 'I am dying, I am denying, I, I . . .'
A shred of the self, an unease: its pleasure
   Would not please the hearer long who heard it

Only within: a violin carries it
  To surrounding air, letting it meet
That first and silent pressure, come
  To test its setting out, its hovering
Over a spun doubt, its own questioning.
  Through a second instrument it flows,
But a third goes counter to it, and a fourth
  Derides both the pride and pains
It has taken to stay proud; and forces,
  Frees it to a singing strength
Until that thread of song, defied,
  Gathering a tributary power, must find
The river course, winding in which
  It can outgo itself—can lose
Not the reality of pain, but that sense
  Of sequestration: the myth of no future
And no ancestry save ache. *Gesang*
  *Ist Dasein?* Song is the measure, rather,
Of being's spread and height, the moonrise
  That tips and touches, recovering from the night
The lost hill-lines, the sleeping prospects:
  It is the will to exchange the graph of pain
Acknowledged, charted and repeated, for the range
  Of an unpredicted terrain. Each phrase
Now follows the undulations of slope, rise
  And drop, released along generous contours
And curving towards a sea where
  The play of light across the dark immensity,
Moves in a shimmering completeness. The tide
  Ridden in unexulting quiet, rides
Up against the craft that sails it
  Tossed and tried, through the groundswell
To the dense calm of unfathomable silence.


# Da Capo

And so
they go back: violin
against piano
to know once more
what it was
they had felt before:

But reapproaching
all they knew
though they touch (almost)
they cannot encroach there:
to know what they knew
and, knowing, seize it,
how should time grow and how
should they reappraise it?

Time beyond all repeal,
they know that they must feel
now what they know,
and going back
to unenterable Eden, they
enter a time new-made
da capo

# THE SHAFT
## (1978)

# Charlotte Corday

O Vertu! le poignard, seul espoir de la terre,
  Est ton arme sacrée ...

                                        Chénier

Courteously self-assured, although alone,
With voice and features that could do no hurt,
Why should she not enter? They let in
A girl whose reading made a heroine—
Her book was Plutarch, her republic Rome:
Home was where she sought her tyrant out.

The towelled head next, the huge batrachian mouth:
There was a mildness in him, even. He
Had never been a woman's enemy,
And time and sickness turned his stomach now
From random execution. All the same,
He moved aside to write her victims down,
And when she approached, it was to kill she came.

She struck him from above. One thrust. Her whole
Intent and innocence directing it
To breach through flesh and enter where it must,
It seemed a blow that rose up from within:
Tinville[1] reduced it all to expertise:
—What, would you make of me a hired assassin?

—What did you find to hate in him?—His crimes.
Every reply was temperate save one
And that was human when all's said and done:
The deposition, read to those who sit
In judgement on her, 'What has she to say?'
'Nothing, except that I succeeded in it.'

—You think that you have killed all Marats off?
—I think perhaps such men are now afraid.
The blade hung in its grooves. How should she know
The Terror still to come, as she was led
Red-smocked from gaol out into evening's red?
It was to have brought peace, that faultless blow.

---

[1] Fonquier Tinville was the public prosecutor.

Uncowed by the unimaginable result,
She loomed by in the cart beneath the eye
Of Danton, Desmoulins and Robespierre,
Heads in a rabble fecund in insult:
She had remade her calendar, called this
The Fourth Day of the Preparation of Peace.

*Greater than Brutus* was what Adam Lux
Demanded for her statue's sole inscription:
His pamphlet was heroic and absurd
And asked the privilege of dying too:
Though the republic raised to her no statue,
The brisk tribunal took him at his word.

What haunted that composure none could fault?
For she, when shown the knife, had dropped her glance—
She 'who believed her death would raise up France'
As Chénier wrote who joined the later dead:
Her judge had asked: 'If you had gone uncaught,
Would you have then escaped?' 'I would,' she said.

A daggered Virtue, Clio's roll of stone,
Action unsinewed into statuary!
Beneath that gaze what tremor was willed down?
And, where the scaffold's shadow stretched its length,
What unlived life would struggle up against
Death died in the possession of such strength?

Perhaps it was the memory of that cry
That cost her most as Catherine Marat
Broke off her testimony . . . But the blade
Inherited the future now and she
Entered a darkness where no irony
Seeps through to move the pity of her shade.

# Marat Dead

The Version of Jacques Louis David

*Citoyen, il suffit que je sois bien malheureuse
pour avoir droit à votre bienveillance.*

Charlotte Corday to Marat

They look like fact, the bath, the wall, the knife,
The splintered packing-case that served as table;
The linen could be priced by any housewife,
As could the weapon too, but not the sable
Suggestion here that colours all we feel
And animates this death-scene from the life
With red, brown, green reflections on the real.

Scaled back to such austerity, each tone
Now sensuous with sadness, would persuade
That in the calm the ugliness has gone
From the vast mouth and from the swaddled head;
And death that worked this metamorphosis
Has left behind no effigy of stone
But wrought an amorous languor with its kiss.

'Citizen, it is enough that I should be
A most unhappy woman to have right
To your benevolence': the heeded plea
Lies on his desk, a patch of bloodied white,
Taking the eye beside the reddening bath,
And single-minded in duplicity,
Loud in the silence of this aftermath.

Words in this painting victimize us all:
Tyro or tyrant, neither shall evade
Such weapons: reader, you grow rational
And miss those sharp intentions that have preyed
On trusting literacy here: unmanned
By generosity and words you fall,
Sprawl forwards bleeding with your pen in hand.

277

She worked in blood, and paint absolves the man,
And in a bathtub laves all previous stains:
She is the dark and absence in the plan
And he a love of justice that remains.
Who was more deft, the painter or the girl?
Marat's best monument with this began,
That all her presence here's a truthless scrawl.


# A Self-Portrait: David

This is the face behind my face. You see
At every trembling touch of paint laid-in
To haunt the ground with shade, enough of me
To tell you what I am. This flesh puts by
The mind's imperious geometry,
The signature of will among the things
That will must change. From this day forth, distrust
Whatever I may do unless it show
A startled truth as in these eyes' misgivings,
These lips that, closed, confess 'I do not know.'


# For Danton

'Bound to the fierce Metropolis . . .'
*The Prelude*, Book X

In the autumn of 1793—the year in which he had instituted the Revolutionary
Tribunal—Danton went back to his birthplace, Arcis-sur-Aube. After his
return in November, he was to be arrested, tried and condemned.

Who is the man that stands against this bridge
And thinks that he and not the river advances?
Can he not hear the links of consequence
Chiming his life away? Water is time.
Not yet, not yet. He fronts the parapet
Drinking the present with unguarded sense:

The stream comes on. Its music deafens him
To other sounds, to past and future wrong.
The beat is regular beneath that song.
He hears in it a pulse that is his own;
He hears the year autumnal and complete.
November waits for him who has not done

With seeings, savourings. Grape-harvest brings
The south into the north. This parapet
Carries him forward still, a ship from Rheims,
From where, in boyhood and on foot, he'd gone
'To see,' he said, 'the way a king is made',
The king that he himself was to uncrown—

Destroyed and superseded, then secure
In the possession of a perfect power
Returned to this: to river, town and plain,
Walked in the fields and knew what power he'd lost,
The cost to him of that metropolis where
He must come back to rule and Robespierre.

Not yet. This contrary perfection he
Must taste into a life he has no time
To live, a lingered, snatched maturity
Before he catches in the waterchime
The measure and the chain a death began,
And fate that loves the symmetry of rhyme
Will spring the trap whose teeth must have a man.

# A Biography of the Author: A Cento

*Or what Rumour and History compounded
concerning the life of the late Sir John Denham
1615–69*

He was born in Dublin, but two years later
before the Foggy Air of that Climate could influence
or any way adulterate his mind,
was brought from thence. Where he went to school
remains uncertain. At Oxford
he continued about three years, being looked upon
as a slow and dreaming young man
and given more to his cards and dice

than to study. After his refusing to pay a debt
to the college recorder and having told him
*I never intended that*
the President rattled him at a lecture in the chapell:
*Thy father the judge* he said *haz hanged
many an honester man.* It was at college
his love of gaming first manifested itself,
and when he had played away all his money
he would play away his father's wrought gold cappes.
At Lincoln's Inn he applied himself
to study the law. As good a student
as any in the house, he was not suspected
to be a witt. Yet he would game much and frequent
the company of gamesters, who rook'd him sometimes
of all he could wrap or get. Generally temperate
as to drink, one time having been merry,
a frolick comes into his head, and with a playsterer's brush
and a pott of inke, he blotted out
all the signes between Temple Barre and Charing-crosse
(this I had from R. Estcott esq. that carried the brush).
When his father objected to his gaming
he wrote, to prove his reformation
and to make sure of his patrimony, *The Anatomy of Play,*
a pamphlet exposing with lucidity
the evils of gaming. At four and twenty
he inherited on the death of the judge, 2 houses well furnished
and much plate, together with numerous estates
in four counties. These were sequestrated
because of his attachment to the king's party.
He aided in the escape of His Majesty, and also of the Duke of
    York—
a person he had much cause to regret later.
He remained faithful to the king
throughout imprisonment, spyings and embassies
between France and England, until
at the Restoration, Charles knighted him
because Denham had 'diverted the evil hour of my banishment'
with his verses. As Royal Surveyor
he knew nothing of architecture,
and would have set the Greenwich Palace
on piles at the very brink of the water. However,
he paved Holborn, being responsible
for the reformation of a thousand deformities in the streets,
the cure of noysom gutters

and the deobstruction of encounters. At fifty
'ancient and limping', he married for a second time. The match
was unequal in many respects, she being twenty-three
and beautiful and soon to become mistress
to the Duke of York. A year later he grew mad,
for having set out to see the free-stone quarries
at Portland in Dorset, he turned back
within a mile of them, and travelled to Hownslowe
to demand rents of the lands he had sold
many years before, thence to the king and told him
he was the Holy Ghost. The king
summoned Valentine Greatrakes, the Irish stroker
who stroked but could not cure him:
a diarist has him for dead, but emended that
to 'not yet dead, but distracted'.
His wife went into Somerset
travelling night and day to see him before he died
and if she could. Sir John was now stark mad
which was occasioned (as is said by some)
by the rough striking of Greatrakes upon his limbs
for they say that having taken the fluxing pills in Holland
and they not working, they rubbed his shins with mercury
but they supposed it lodged in the nerves
till the harsh strokes caused it to sublimate.
This was in April 1666:
By September 'that great master of wit and reason'
no longer mad, but still noticeably eccentric,
has returned to Parliament, a member of various committees
and in regular attendance. My Lord Lisle writes:
'If he had not the name of being mad, I believe
in most companies he would be thought wittier
than ever he was. He has few extravagances besides that
of telling stories of himself, which he is always inclined to
and some of his acquaintances say that extreme vanity
was the cause of his madness, as it was the effect.'
There is little doubt that the cause of his madness
was youthful venery, but opinion attributed it
to his being a notorious cuckold at the hands
of the Duke of York, he going at noon-day with all his gentlemen
to visit my Lady Denham
in Scotland Yard, she declaring
she will not be his mistresse to go up and down the privy-stairs
but will be owned publicly; and so she is. Mr Evelyn
calls it bitchering, for the Duke of York

talks a little to her, and then she goes away,
and then he follows her again like a dog. In November
on the afternoon of the tenth
my Lady Denham is exceeding sick, even to death,
she saying and everyone else discoursing
that she is poysoned, but the physicians affirm
the cause of her sickness to have been
*iliaca passio.* At the turn of the year
my Lady Denham is at last dead,
but when the body was opened, the autopsy
revealed no trace of poison, though could not check
the persistence of contrary rumour, some
alleging it was administered in a cup of chocolate,
others that the Duchess of York had accomplished her death
with a powder of diamond, or that 'Old Denham'
being jealous and having no country house
to which he could carry his unfortunate wife
had made her travel a much longer journey
without stirring from London. The populace
had a design of tearing him in pieces
as soon as he should come abroad, but was appeased
by the magnificence of the funeral where he distributed
four times more burnt wine
than ever had been drunk at any burial in England—
soon afterwards, the Duchess of York
troubled with the appearance of the Lady Denham
bit off a piece of her tongue. Denham
in the ensuing quiet
and profiting by the remission of his disease
wrote one of his best pieces, the eulogy of Cowley,
but on account of his weakness
was forced to appoint Wren
Deputy Surveyor. He did not survive
his wife or his poem long, but died at his office
probably of an apoplexy
two years after her death. As to the disposition of his body
there was some hesitation:
What means this silence that may seeme to doome
Denham to an undistinguished tomb
wrote Mr Christopher Wase, but 'loath'd oblivion
and neglect' being averted, he was buried
in the Abbey.

# Lines Written in the Euganean Hills

1

The tiles of the swimming pool are azure,
   Dyeing on breast and wings the swifts
That, transfigured, hunt its surface:
   This is man's landscape, all transfigurings
Across the thrust of origin—of rock
   Under schists and clays, their erratic
Contours cross-ruled by vine on vine:
   Over the table, flies are following-out the stains
Tasting the man-made, the mature stale wine.

2

An aridity haunts the edges of the fields:
   The irrigation jet, irising, arching
Across the cloud of its own wet smoke,
   Puts a gloss on the crop. But the cricket
Is raucous, the hoarse voice of that dust
   That whitening the grassroots of the burnt-out ditches,
Has webbed-over the spider's net with chalk.

3

Unshuttering vistas
mournfully the wizened
female custodian recites
snatches of Petrarch
whose statue cramped
in the cellarage gesticulates
beside his mummified cat, Laura.

4

D'Annunzio saw it all behind golden mist,
A wavering of decay, vegetable, vast,
That had taken hold on each statue, each relief,
And was eating and unmaking them, as if leaf by leaf.
Two wars, and the mathematic of the humanist
Re-declares itself in white persistence,
Slogans scaling the plinths and walls where Mao
And Lenin dispute the Palladian ratio.

## Death in Venice

Glass gauds from Murano.
The band at Florian's are drowsing
drowned in the syrup of their rhapsody.
A high stack
flaring-off waste from Mestre
hangs beaconed across water
where each outboard's wake
is flexing, unmaking those marble
images, bridals of stone
and sea, restless to have
that piled longevity
down and done.

## Near Corinium

The recalcitrance
                    of whorl-wheel fossils
of belemnite teeth
                    shatterings
from the meteors
                    gods had hurled
according
            to those who also
lie in the subsoil these inlay:
            'I, Caius Martius restored
                this Jupiter column
                the Christians had defaced'
                                    of which
only the limestone base . . .
                            those who,
these which—
                history's particles refusing
both completion
                    and extinction:
traceries
        finer than the lines
of spider floss:
                it is as though
this torn tapestry
                    faded calligraphy

284

were whole
                    if only one could adjust
one's eyes to them:
                         excavations
for the by-pass:
                    the dust-motes turning like stars
which the air-currents lift


## Near York

The glistening field has survived its battles:
    A fault in the window-pane takes hold,
Twists to a dip the plain of York:
    But at one shift of the eye the straight
Flows back to occupy that hollow,
    Shadows following ditch and field-line
In horizontals. It is no tyranny
    To the cycle a hedge hides and whose rider
Slotted into the scene, drifts by
    And, making the will of the land his own,
Is wing-swift land-bound. Birds alone
    Can seem to defy the law of the plain:
The lapwings shape out of nothing
    The fells they come dropping through; and their hills
Of air roll with the currents of a wind
    Calling to York from Jorvik as it tries
To speak through this casement where a fault in glass
    Keeps rippling and releasing tense horizons;
As if this place could be pried out of now,
    As if we could fly in the face of all we know.


## Casarola

### for Attilio Bertolucci

Cliffs come sheering down into woodland here:
    The trees—they are chestnuts—spread to a further drop
Where an arm of water rushes through unseen
    Still lost in leaves: you can hear it
Squandering its way towards the mill
    A path crossing a hillslope and a bridge

Leads to at last: the stones lie there
   Idle beside it: they were cut from the cliff
And the same stone rises in wall and roof
   Not of the mill alone, but of shed on shed
Whose mossed tiles like a city of the dead
   Grow green in the wood. There are no dead here
And the living no longer come
   In October to crop the trees: the chestnuts
Dropping, feed the roots they rose from:
   A rough shrine sanctifies the purposes
These doors once opened to, a desolation
   Of still-perfect masonry. There is a beauty
In this abandonment: there would be more
   In the slow activity of smoke
Seeping at roof and lintel; out of each low
   Unwindowed room rising to fill
Full with essences the winter wood
   As the racked crop dried. Waste
Is our way. An old man
   Has been gathering mushrooms. He pauses
To show his spoil, plumped by a soil
   Whose sweet flour goes unmilled:
Rapid and unintelligible, he thinks we follow
   As we feel for his invitations to yes and no:
Perhaps it's the mushrooms he's telling over
   Or this place that shaped his dialect, and where nature
Daily takes the distinctness from that signature
   Men had left there in stone and wood,
Among waning villages, above the cities of the plain.


## Portobello Carnival 1973


A malleability
            a precision
with which they keep the beat
                        their bodies
overflowing to the house-doors
                        dancing
so that the street
            is a jostled conduit
that contains them (just):
                  the steel-band ride,

their pace decided
                    by the crowd's pace
before their open truck
                    to a music
of detritus
           wheelhubs, cans:
the tempered oil-drums
                        yield a Caribbean sweetness
belied by the trumpet
                    that gliding on
ahead of the ostinato
                    divides
what the beat unites:
                    the trumpeter knows
and through his breath
                        and fingers the knowledge
flows into acid sound:
                    you will not go back
to the fronds, the sands
                        Windward, Leeward
and all those islands
                    the banner bears forward
under the promise
                FOREVER:
below
     human peacocks and imaginary birds,
a devil
       hoisting as a flag
his black bat-wings
                    that have come unpinned (unpinioned):
in all the sweat
                and garish conglomeration of dress
there is a rightness
                    to every acrylic splash
spattering the London grey,
                            the unrelenting trumpet deriding
the drum-beat fable
                    of a tribal content
on this day of carnival,
                        the dissonance
half-assuaged in the sway of flesh
                                holding back time
dancing off history.

# *Prose Poem*

### *for John and Lisbeth*

If objects are of two kinds—those
    That we contemplate and, the remainder, use,
I am unsure whether its poetry or prose
    First drew us to this jar. A century
Ago, an apothecary must have been its owner,
    Thankful that it was airtight. And in spite of time
It remains so still. Its cylinder of glass,
    Perfectly seamless, has the finality and satisfaction
Of the achieved act of an artisan. Indeed,
    The stopper of ground glass, that refused
To be freed from the containing neck,
    Was almost too well-made. What had to be done
If we were to undo it, was to pass
    A silk cord round the collar of glass
And rub it warm—but this friction
    Must be swift enough not to conduct its heat
Inside—the best protection against which
    (Only a third hand can ensure this feat)
Is a cube of ice on top of the stopper.
    Whether it was the rubbing only, or the warm
Grasp that must secure the bottle's body,
    The stopper, once more refusing at first,
Suddenly parted—breathed-out
    (So to speak) by the warmed expanding glass.
Remaining ice-cool itself, when
    Lightly oiled, it was now ready again
For use—but not before we had tried
    Jar against ear to find the sound inside it.
It gave off—no seashell murmur—
    A low, crystalline roar that wholly
Possessed one's cavities, a note (as it were)
    Of unfathomable distance—not emptiness,
For this dialogue between air and ear
    Was so full of electric imponderables, it could compare
Only with that molecular stealth when the jar
    Had breathed. There is one sole lack
Now that jar and stopper are in right relation—
    An identifiable aroma: what we must do
Is to fill it with coffee, for use, scent and contemplation.

# Departure

You were to leave and being all but gone,
   Turned on yourselves, to see that stream
Which bestows a flowing benediction and a name
   On our house of stone. Late, you had time
For a glance, no more, to renew your sense
   Of how the brook—in spate now—
Entered the garden, pooling, then pushing
   Over a fall, to sidle a rock or two
Before it was through the confine. Today,
   The trail of your jet is scoring the zenith
Somewhere, and I, by the brink once more,
   Can tell you now what I had to say
But didn't then: it is here
   That I like best, where the waters disappear
Under the bridge-arch, shelving through coolness,
   Thought, halted at an image of perfection
Between gloom and gold, in momentary
   Stay, place of perpetual threshold,
Before all flashes out again and on
   Tasseling and torn, reflecting nothing but sun.

# Images of Perfection

            . . . What do we see
   In the perfect thing? Is our seeing
Merely a measuring, a satisfaction
   To be compared? How do we know at sight
And for what they are, these rarenesses
   That are right? In yesterday's sky
Every variety of cloud accompanied earth,
   Mares' tails riding past mountainous anvils,
While their shadows expunged our own:
   It was pure display—all a sky could put on
In a single day, and yet remain sky.
   I mean, you felt in the air the sway
Of sudden apocalypse, complete revelation:
   But what it came to was a lingering
At the edge of time, a perfect neighbouring,
   Until the twilight brought it consummation,
Seeping in violet through the entire scene.

Where was the meaning, then? Did Eden
Greet us ungated? Or was that marrying
    Purely imaginary and, if it were,
What do we see in the perfect thing?


# Rhymes


Perfect is the word I can never hear
    Without a sensation as of seeing—
As though a place should grow perfectly clear,
    The light on the look of it agreeing
To show—not all there is to be seen,
    But all you would wish to know
At a given time. Word and world rhyme
    As the penstrokes might if you drew
The spaciousness reaching down through a valley view,
    Gathering the lines into its distances
As if they were streams, as if they were eye-beams:
    Perfect, then, the eye's command in its riding,
Perfect the coping hand, the hillslopes
    Drawing it into such sight the sight would miss,
Guiding the glance the way perfection is.


# The Perfection


There is that moment when,
the sun almost gone,
red gains and deepens on
neighbouring cloud:

and the shadows that seam
and grain it take
to themselves
indelible black:

yet we never know it
until it has been
for the moment it is
and the next has brought in

a lost pitch,
a lack-lustre pause
in the going glow
where the perfection was.


# The Hesitation

Spring lingers-out its arrival in these woods:
    A generation of flowers has been and gone
Before one tree has put on half its leaves:
    A butterfly wavers into flight yet scarcely wakes:
Chill currents of the air it tries to ride
    Cannot fulfill the promises of the sun
To favoured coverts sheltered beneath a hillside:
    Is it may blossom smokes on the thicket crest,
Or the pallor of hoar-frost whitening its last?


# The Faring

That day, the house was so much a ship
    Clasped by the wind, the whole sky
Piling its cloud-wrack past,
    To be sure you were on dry land
You must go out and stand in that stream
    Of air: the entire world out there
Was travelling too: in each gap the tides
    Of space felt for the earth's ship sides:
Over fields, new-turned, the cry
    And scattered constellations of the gulls
Were messengers from that unending sea, the sky:
    White on brown, a double lambency
Pulsed, played where the birds, intent
    On nothing more than the ploughland's nourishment,
Brought the immeasurable in: wing on wing
    Taking new lustres from the turning year
Above seasonable fields, they tacked and climbed
    With a planet's travelling, rhymed here with elsewhere
In the sea-salt freshnesses of tint and air.

# The Metamorphosis

Bluebells come crowding a fellside
   A stream once veined. It rises
Like water again where, bell on bell,
   They flow through its bed, each rope
And rivulet, each tributary thread
   Found-out by flowers. And not the slope
Alone, runs with this imaginary water:
   Marshes and pools of it stay
On the valley-floor, fed (so the eye would say)
   From the same store and streamhead.
Like water, too, this blueness not all blue
   Goes ravelled with groundshades, grass and stem,
As the wind dishevels and strokes it open;
   So that the mind, in salutory confusion,
Surrendering up its powers to the illusion,
   Could, swimming in metamorphoses, believe
Water itself might move like a flowing of flowers.


# Below Tintern

The river's mirrorings remake a world
   Green to the cliff-tops, hanging
Wood by wood, towards its counterpart:
   Green gathers there as no green could
That water did not densen. Yet why should mind
   So eagerly swim down and through
Such towering dimness? Because that world seems true?
   And yet it could not, if it were,
Suspend more solid castles in the air.
   Machicolations, look-outs for mind's eye
Feed and free it with mere virtuality
   Where the images elude us. For they are true enough
Set wide with invitation where they lie
   Those liquid thresholds, that inverted sky
Gripped beneath rockseams by the valley verdure,
   Lost to reflection as the car bends by.

# Providence

It is May: 'A bad winter,'
  They prophesy, the old women—they
Who remember still—for I cannot—
  Years when the hawthorns were as thick as now:
Spray on spray hangs over
  In heavy flounces, white swags
Weigh down the pliancy of branches,
  Drag at a whole tree until it bends:
I thought it must be these snow-brides, snow-ghosts
  Brought-on their unseasonable dream of frosts:
But old women know the blossoms must give way
  To berry after berry, as profuse as they,
On which, come winter, the birds will feed:
  For what in the world could justify and bring
Inexplicable plenty if not the birds' need?—
  And winter must be harsh for appetite
Such as they have the means now to requite:
  Old women reason providentially
From other seasons, remembering how
  Winter set out to hunt the sparrows down
In years when the hawthorns were as thick as now.

# Mushrooms

### for Jon and Jill

Eyeing the grass for mushrooms, you will find
A stone or stain, a dandelion puff
Deceive your eyes—their colour is enough
To plump the image out to mushroom size
And lead you through illusion to a rind
That's true—flint, fleck or feather. With no haste
Scent-out the earthy musk, the firm moist white,
And, played-with rather than deluded, waste
None of the sleights of seeing: taste the sight
You gaze unsure of—a resemblance, too,
Is real and all its likes and links stay true
To the weft of seeing. You, to begin with,
May be taken in, taken beyond, that is,
This place of chiaroscuro that seemed clear,

For realer than a myth of clarities
Are the meanings that you read and are not there:
Soon, in the twilight coolness, you will come
To the circle that you seek and, one by one,
Stooping into their fragrance, break and gather,
Your way a winding where the rest lead on
Like stepping stones across a grass of water.


## In the Intensity of Final Light

In the intensity of final light
　　Deepening, dyeing, moss on the tree-trunks
Glares more green than the foliage they bear:
　　Hills, then, have a way of taking fire
To themselves as though they meant to hold
　　In a perpetuity of umber, amber, gold
Those forms that, by the unstable light of day,
　　Refuse all final outline, drift
From a dew-cold blue into green-shot grey:
　　In the intensity of final light
A time of loomings, then a chime of lapses
　　Failing from woodslopes, summits, sky,
Leaving, for the moonrise to untarnish,
　　Hazed airy fastnesses where the last rays vanish.


## The Spring Symphony

This is the Spring Symphony. Schumann
　　Wrote it in autumn. Now it is June.
Nothing to deny, nothing to identify
　　The season of this music. Autumn in the cellos
Is proverbial, yet these consent
　　To be the perfect accompaniment to such a day
As now declares itself: on the flexed grass
　　New sheen: the breeze races in it
Blent with light as on the face of waters:
　　The returning theme—new earth, new sky—
Filled the orchestral universe until,
　　On fire to be fleshed-out, leaf and seed
Became their dream and dazzle in freshness still:
　　Yet, self-consuming, these

Emanations, energies that press
   In light and wind to their completeness,
Seem half irate: invaded by this music
   The summer's single theme might be
The mind's own rage against mortality
   In wasting, hastening flight towards
The sum of all, the having done.
   This summer sound is the Spring Symphony
Written in autumn. Death is its ground,
   Life hurrying to death, its urgency,
Its timelessness, its melody and wound.


# Nature Poem

This August heat, this momentary breeze,
First filtering through, and then prolonged in it,
Until you feel the two as one, this sound
Of water that is sound of leaves, they all
In stirrings and comminglings so recall
The ways a poem flows, they ask to be
Written into a permanence—not stilled
But given pulse and voice. So many shades,
So many filled recesses, stones unseen
And daylight darknesses beneath the trees,
No single reading renders up complete
Their shifting text—a poem, too, in this,
They bring the mind half way to its defeat,
Eluding and exceeding the place it guesses,
Among these overlappings, half-lights, depths,
The currents of this air, these hiddenesses.


# The Whip

We are too much on the outside
in the inside of the ear
to sort clear at first
the unrolling of the thunder: then
deserting the distances, all
that sunken mumbling turns
to a spine of sound, a celestial
whipline, the crack at the end

of each lash implied under the first
spreading salvo the ears
had been merely fumbling with:
one sky-track now
flashes through them as keen
as the lightning dancing to the eye
the shape of the whip that woke
in them its uncoiling soundscape.


## To See the Heron

To see the heron rise
detaching blue from the blue
that, smoking, lies along
field–hollows, shadowings
of humidity: to see it
set off that blaze
where ranks of autumn trees
are waiting just for this
raised torch, this touch,
this leisurely sideways
wandering ascension to unite
their various brightnesses, their fire-
music as a voice might
riding sound: risen
it is darkening now
against the sullen sky blue,
so let it go
unaccompanied save by the thought
that this is autumn and the stream
whose course its eye is travelling
the source of fish: to see the heron
hang wondering where
to stoop, to alight and strike.


## One Day of Autumn

One day of autumn
sun had uncongealed
the frost that clung
wherever shadows spread

their arctic greys among
October grass: mid-
field an oak still
held its foliage intact
but then began
releasing leaf by leaf
full half,
till like a startled
flock they scattered
on the wind: and one
more venturesome than all
the others shone far out
a moment in mid-air,
before it glittered off
and sheered into the dip
a stream ran through
to disappear with it

## October

Autumn seems ending: there is lassitude
Wherever ripeness has not filled its brood
Of rinds and rounds: all promises are fleshed
Or now they fail. Far gone, these blackberries—
For each one that you pull, two others fall
Full of themselves, the leaves slick with their ooze:
Awaiting cold, we welcome in the frost
To cleanse these purples, this discandying,
As eagerly as we shall look to spring.

## Old Man's Beard

What we failed to see
was twines of the wild clematis
climbing all summer
through each burdened tree:

not till the leaves were gone
did we begin to take
the measure of what strength
had fed from the limestone

that roof of feathered seed
bearding the woods now
in its snowy foliage
yet before fall of snow

and what silent cordage bound
the galaxy together where
December light reflected
from star on hairy star

innumerably united
in a cascade, a cloud, a wing
to hang their canopy above
the roots they were strangling.


## . . . *Or Traveller's Joy*

I return late
on a wintry road: the beam
has suddenly lit
flowers of frost, or so they seem:

Traveller's Joy! the recognition
flares as soon, almost,
as the headlights quit
those ghosts of petals:

a time returns, when men
fronting the winter starkness
were travellers travailing
against hail, mud, dark:

then, whoever it was,
much road behind him,
coming, perhaps, at dawn
with little to remind him

he was cared for, kinned,
saw from the road
the hedgerow loaded
and thought it rimed:

and so it was: the name
he drew from that sudden brightness
came as if his joy
were nature's, too:

and the sweet illusion
persists with the name
into present night,
under the travelling beam.

## In the Balance

The cold came. It has photographed the scene
With so exact a care, that you can look
From field-white and from wood-black to the air
Now that the snow has ceased, and catch no shade
Except these three—the third is the sky's grey:
Will it thicken or thaw, this rawness menacing?
The sky stirs: the sky refuses to say:
But it lets new colour in: its thinning smoke
Opens towards a region beyond snow,
Rifts to a blueness rather than a blue:
Brought to a sway, the whole day hesitates
Through the sky of afternoon, and you beneath,
As if questions of weather were of life and death.

## The Death of Will

The end was more of a melting:
as if frost turned heavily to dew
and the flags, dragged down by it,
clung to their poles: marble becoming glue.

Alive, no one had much cared
for Will: Will no sooner gone,
there was a *je ne sais quoi*, a *ton*
'fell from the air':

And how strange that, Will once dead,
Passion must die, too,
although they'd had nothing to do
with each other, so it was said:

299

It was then everyone stopped looking
for the roots of decay,
for curative spears and chapels perilous
and the etymology of 'heyday':

Parents supine, directionless,
looked to their wilful children now:
was this metempsychosis?
was Will reborn in them somehow?

Someone should record Will's story.
Someone should write a book on *Will and Zen*.
Someone should trace all those who
knew Will, to interview them. Someone

# A Night at the Opera

When the old servant reveals she is the mother
  Of the young count whose elder brother
Has betrayed him, the heroine, disguised
  As the Duke's own equerry, sings *Or'*
*Che sono*, pale from the wound she has received
  In the first act. The entire court
Realize what has in fact occurred and wordlessly
  The waltz song is to be heard now
In the full orchestra. And we, too,
  Recall that meeting of Marietta with the count
Outside the cloister in Toledo. She faints:
  Her doublet being undone, they find
She still has on the hair-shirt
  Worn ever since she was a nun
In Spain. So her secret is plainly out
  And Boccaleone (blind valet
To the Duke) confesses it is he (*Or' son'io*)
  Who overheard the plot to kidnap the dead
Count Bellafonte, to burn by night
  The high camp of the gipsy king
Alfiero, and by this stratagem quite prevent
  The union of both pairs of lovers.
Now the whole cast packs the stage
  Raging in chorus round the quartet—led
By Alfiero (having shed his late disguise)
  And Boccaleone (shock has restored his eyes):

Marietta, at the first note from the count
  (Long thought dead, but finally revealed
As Alfiero), rouses herself, her life
  Hanging by a thread of song, and the Duke,
Descending from his carriage to join in,
  Dispenses pardon, punishment and marriage.
Exeunt to the Grand March, Marietta
  (Though feebly) marching, too, for this
Is the 'Paris' version where we miss
  The ultimate dénouement when at the command
Of the heroine (*Pura non son'*) Bellafonte marries
  The daughter of the gipsy king and

## *In the Studio*

'Recorded ambience'—this
is what they call
silences put back
between the sounds:
leaves might fall
on to the roof-glass to compound
an instant ambience
from the drift of sibilants:
but winter boughs
cannot enter—they
distort like weed
under the glass water:
this (sifted) silence
now recording (one
minute only of it)
comprises what
you did not hear before
you began to listen—
the sighs that
in a giant building
rise up trapped between
its sound-proofed surfaces
murmuring, replying
to themselves, gathering
power like static

from the atmosphere: you do
hear this ambience?
it rings true: for silence
is an imagined thing.


# *Misprint*

### *for L.S. Dembo*

'Meeting' was what
I had intended:
'melting' ended
an argument that
should have led
out (as it were)
into a clearing, an
amphitheatre
civic or sylvan
where what could not be
encompassed stood
firmly encompassing
column on column, tree on tree
in their clear ring:
there I had hoped to come
into my true
if transitory kingdom:
instead, one
single letter has un-
made, punned
meaning away into
a statuary circle
becoming snow
and down I dissolve with it
statue on statue
gobbet on slithering gobbet

# Maintenant

### for Samuel Menashe

Hand
holding on to this
instant metamorphosis,
the syllables maintain
against the lapse
of time that they remain
here, where all else escapes


# Sky Writing

A plane goes by,
and the sky takes hold
on the frail, high chalk-line
of its vapour-trail, picks
it apart, combs out
and spreads the filaments
down either side
the spine of a giant plume
which rides written on air now:
that flocculent, unwieldy sceptre
begins its sway with
an essential uncertainty, a
veiled threat tottering it
slowly to ruin, and the sky
grasping its tatters
teases them thin,
letting in blue until,
all flaxen cobblings, lit
transparencies, they
give up their ghosts
to air, lost in their opposite.

## Into Distance

Swift cloud
across still cloud
drifting east
so that the still
seems also on the move
the other way: a vast
opposition throughout the sky
and, as one stands
watching the separating
gauzes, greys, the eyes
wince dizzily away from them:
feeling for roots anew
one senses the strength
in planted legs, the pull
at neck, tilted
upwards to a blue that
ridding itself of all
its drift keeps now
only those few, still
island clouds to occupy
its oceanic spread
where a single, glinting plane
bound on and over
is spinning into distance and ahead
of its own sound

## Embassy

A breeze keeps fleshing the flag:
  I watch it droop, then reassemble
On air an emblem I do not know:
  Nor does that woman know the part
She plays in this rhymescheme that no art
  Has prompted: for the breeze begins
Feeling along the dyed silk of her hair,
  Unfurling its viking platinum to the same
Rhythm with which the flag bursts into flame:
  Steam seeps from a manhole in the asphalt:
And that, too, leans to the common current,

Goes upward taking shape from the unseen
In this unpremeditable action where
A wind is having its way with all swayable things,
Combing through flag and steam, streaming-out hair.


# The Race

These waters run secretively until
    Rushing the race where a mill stood once
The weight comes drumming down,
    Crushing-out whiteness as they fall
And fill with a rocking yeast this pool
    They clamour across: clamour and clamber
Blindly till again they find their leat
    And level, narrow-out into
A now-smooth riverlane and pouring on
    Go gathering up the silence where they run.


# In Arden

'This is the forest of Arden . . .'

Arden is not Eden, but Eden's rhyme:
    Time spent in Arden is time at risk
And place, also: for Arden lies under threat:
    Ownership will get what it can for Arden's trees:
No acreage of green-belt complacencies
    Can keep Macadam out: Eden lies guarded:
Pardonable Adam, denied its gate,
    Walks the grass in a less-than-Eden light
And whiteness that shines from a stone burns with his fate:
    Sun is tautening the field's edge shadowline
Along the wood beyond: but the contraries
    Of this place are contrarily unclear:
A haze beats back the summer sheen
    Into a chiaroscuro of the heat:
The down on the seeded grass that beards
    Each rise where it meets with sky,
Ripples a gentle fume: a fine
    Incense, smelling of hay smokes by:
Adam in Arden tastes its replenishings:
    Through its dense heats the depths of Arden's springs

Convey echoic waters—voices
  Of the place that rises through this place
Overflowing, as it brims its surfaces
  In runes and hidden rhymes, in chords and keys
Where Adam, Eden, Arden run together
  And time itself must beat to the cadence of this river.


## The Roe Deer

We must anticipate the dawn one day,
Crossing the long field silently to see
The roe deer feed. Should there be snow this year
Taking their tracks, searching their colours out,
The dusk may help us to forestall their doubt
And drink the quiet of their secrecy
Before, the first light lengthening, they are gone.
One day we must anticipate the dawn.


## The Shaft

### for Guy Davenport

The shaft seemed like a place of sacrifice:
  You climbed where spoil heaps from the hill
Spilled out into a wood, the slate
  Tinkling underfoot like shards, and then
You bent to enter: a passageway:
  Cervix of stone: the tick of waterdrops,
A clear clepsydra: and squeezing through
  Emerged into cathedral space, held-up
By a single rocksheaf, a gerbe
  Buttressing-back the roof. The shaft
Opened beneath it, all its levels
  Lost in a hundred feet of water.
Those miners—dust, beards, mattocks—
  They photographed seventy years ago,
Might well have gone to ground here, pharoahs
  Awaiting excavation, their drowned equipment
Laid-out beside them. All you could see
  Was rock reflections tunneling the floor
That water covered, a vertical unfathomed,

A vertigo that dropped through centuries
To the first who broke into these fells:
    The shaft was not a place to stare into
Or not for long: the adit you entered by
    Filtered a leaf-light, a phosphorescence,
Doubled by water to a tremulous fire
    And signalling you back to the moist door
Into whose darkness you had turned aside
    Out of the sun of an unfinished summer.


## *De Sole*

*after Ficino*
*(for Homero Aridjis)*

If once a year
the house of the dead
stood open
and those dwelling
under its roof
were shown the world's
great wonders, all
would marvel beyond every other thing at
the sun


## *Macduff*

This wet sack, wavering slackness
    They drew out silent through the long
Blood-edged incision, this black
    Unbreathing thing they must first
Hoist from a beam by its heels and swing
    To see whether it could yet expel
Death through each slimy nostril,
    This despaired-of, half-born mishap
Shuddered into a live calf, knew
    At a glance mother, udder and what it must do
Next and did it, mouthing for milk.
    The cow, too, her womb stitched back inside,
Her hide laced up, leans down untaught
    To lick clean her untimely firstborn:

'Pity it's a male.' She looms there innocent
  That words have meanings, but long ago
This blunt lapsarian instinct, poetry,
  Found life's sharpest, readiest
Rhyme, unhesitating—it was knife—
  By some farm-yard gate, perhaps,
That led back from nature into history.

## Tree

I took a tree for a guide—I mean
  Gazing sideways, I had chosen idly
Over walls, fields and other trees,
  This single elm, or it had chosen me:
At all events, it so held my mind,
  I did not stop to admire as otherwise I should
The charlock all in yellow fire against
  A sky of thunder-grey: I walked on,
Taking my bearings from that trunk
  And, as I moved, the tree moved too
Alongside, or it seemed to do. Seemed?
  Incontrovertibly the intervening hedgerows occupied
Their proper place, a mid-ground
  In a bounded scene, myopically vague
At each extremity. But the elm
  Paced as if parallel for half a mile
Before I could outstrip it and consign
  The sight into the distances. A trick
Of the eye no doubt, but one not easily
  Put out of mind: that branch-crowned tower,
That stalking memorial of Dunsinane
  Reared alien there, but it was I
Was the stranger on that silent field,
  Gazing unguarded, guideless at a frontier
I could never cross nor whose image raze.

## The Gap

It could be that you are driving by.
  You do not need the whole of an eye
To command the thing: the edge
  Of a merely desultory look

Will take it in—it is a gap
    (No more) where you'd expect to see
A field-gate, and there well may be
    But it is flung wide, and the land so lies
All you see is space—that, and the wall
    That climbs up to the spot two ways
To embrace absence, frame skies:
    Why does one welcome the gateless gap?
As an image to be filled with the meaning
    It doesn't yet have? As a confine gone?
A saving grace in so much certainty of stone?
    Reason can follow reason, one by one.
But the moment itself, abrupt
    With the pure surprise of seeing,
Will outlast all after-knowledge and its map—
    Even, and perhaps most then, should the unseen
Gate swing-to across that gap.

## *The Scream*

Night. A dream so drowned my mind,
    Slowly it rose towards that sound,
Hearing no scream in it, but a high
    Thin note, such as wasp or fly
Whines-out when spider comes dancing down
    To inspect its net. Curtains—
I dragged them back—muffled the cry:
    It rang in the room, but I could find
No web, wasp, fly. Blackly
    Beyond the pane, the same sound
Met the ear and, whichever way
    You pried for its source, seemed to be everywhere.
Torch, stair, door: the black
    Was wavering in the first suffusion
Of the small hours' light. But nothing
    Came clearly out of that obscure
Past-midnight, unshaped world, except
    The shrill of this savaging. I struck uphill
And, caught in the torchbeam, saw
    A lustre of eye, a dazzle on tooth
And stripe: badger above its prey
    Glared worrying at that strident thing

It could neither kill nor silence. It swung
　　Round to confront the light and me,
Sinewed, it seemed, for the attack, until
　　I flung at it, stoned it back
And away from whatever it was that still
　　Screamed on, hidden in greyness. A dream
Had delivered me to this, and a dream
　　Once more seemed to possess one's mind,
For light could not find an embodiment for that scream,
　　Though it found the very spot and tussock
That relentlessly breathed and heaved it forth.
　　Was it a sound half-underground? Would badger
Bury its prey? Thoughts like these
　　No thoughts at all, crowded together
To appall the mind with dream uncertainties.
　　I flashed at the spot. It took reason
To unknot the ravel that hindered thought,
　　And reason could distinguish what was there,
But could no more bear the cry
　　Than the untaught ear. It was the tussock lived
And turned, now, at the touch of sight
　　—You could eye the lice among its spines—
To a hedgehog. Terrible in the denial
　　Of all comfort, it howled on here
For the lease that was granted it, the life
　　That was safe, and which it could not feel
Was its own yet. It howled down death
　　So that death might meet with its equal
Ten times the size of the despised life
　　It had hunted for. In this comedy
Under the high night, this refusal
　　To die with a taciturn, final dignity
A wolf's death, the scream
　　In its nest of fleas took on the sky.


# Translating the Birds

The buzzard's two-note cry falls plaintively,
　　And, like a seabird's, hesitates between
A mewing, a regret, a plangent plea,
　　Or so we must translate it who have never
Hung with the buzzard or above the sea.

It veers a haughty circle with sun-caught breast:
  The small birds are all consternation now,
And do not linger to admire the sight,
  The flash of empery that solar fire
Lends to the predatory ease of flight.

The small birds have all taken to the trees,
  Their eyes alert, their garrulousness gone:
Beauty does not stir them, realists to a man,
  They know what awe's exacted by a king,
They know that now is not the time to sing.

They'll find their way back into song once more
  Who've only sung in metaphor and we
Will credit them with arias, minstrelsy,
  And, eager always for the intelligible,
Instruct those throats what meaning they must tell.

But supply pulsing, wings against the air,
  With yelp that bids the silence of small birds,
Now it is the buzzard owns the sky
  Thrusting itself beyond the clasp of words,
Word to dance with, dally and outfly.

## *The Scar*

That night, the great tree split
  Where it forked, and a full half lay
At morning, prone by the other
  To await decay. The scar
Of cleavage gleams along the trunk
  With such a tall and final whiteness,
It is the living tree seems dead
  That rears from its own done life
Preparing to put on leaf. Buds
  Bead and soon the leaves will cover
That sapless-seeming wintershape all over.
  A debris clings there and claws
At the tree-foot, spills out
  Up half a hill in bone-white antlerings:
Over it all, the scar glints down,
  And a spring light pulsating ashen,
You would swear that through the shuddered trunk
  Still tremors the memory of its separation.

# *At Dawn*

*in memoriam F.M.D.*

The blue took you, a wing of ash:
    Returning from the summit where
We had released you into the sky
    And air of earliest day, we saw
Deer at gaze, deer drinking
    Before the blaze of desert sun
Dispersed them: that liquid look
    So held us, it was less a thing
Consolatory than a fact of morning,
    Its freshness returning us to time,
Its farness acknowledging the claim
    Of such distance as we shall only know
On a wing of ash, absorbed against the blue.

# THE FLOOD
## (1981)

# Snow Signs

They say it is waiting for more, the snow
  Shrunk up to the shadow-line of walls
In an arctic smouldering, an unclean salt,
  And will not go until the frost returns
Sharpening the stars, and the fresh snow falls
  Piling its drifts in scallops, furls. I say
Snow has left its own white geometry
  To measure out for the eye the way
The land may lie where a too cursory reading
  Discovers only dip and incline leading
To incline, dip, and misses the fortuitous
  Full variety a hillside spreads for us:
It is written here in sign and exclamation,
  Touched-in contour and chalk-followed fold,
Lines and circles finding their completion
  In figures less certain, figures that yet take hold
On features that would stay hidden but for them:
  Walking, we waken these at every turn,
Waken ourselves, so that our walking seems
  To rouse some massive sleeper out of winter dreams
Whose stretching startles the whole land into life,
  As if it were us the cold, keen signs were seeking
To pleasure and remeasure, repossess
  With a sense in the gathered coldness of heat and height.
Well, if it's for more the snow is waiting
  To claim back into disguisal overnight,
As though it were promising a protection
  From all it has transfigured, scored and bared,
Now we shall know the force of what resurrection
  Outwaits the simplification of the snow.


# Their Voices Rang

Their voices rang
through the winter trees:
they were speaking and yet it seemed they sang,
the trunks a hall of victory.

And what is that and where?
Though we come to it rarely,
the sense of all that we might be
conjures the place from air.

Is it the mind, then?
It is the mind received,
assumed into a season
forestial in the absence of all leaves.

Their voices rang
through the winter trees and time
catching the cadence of that song
forgot itself in them.


## The Double Rainbow

*To Ulalume Gonzalez de Leon*

When I opened your book
a rainbow shaft
looked into it
through the winter window:

a January light
searching the pane
paused there refracted
from white onto white:

so words become
brides of the weather
of the day in the room
and the day outside:

in the light of the mind
the meanings loom
to dance in their own
glimmering spectrum

# For Miriam

## I

I climbed to your high village through the snow,
   Stepping and slipping over lost terrain:
Wind having stripped a dead field of its white
   Had piled the height beyond: I saw no way
But hung there wrapped in breath, my body beating:
   Edging the drift, trying it for depth.
Touch taught the body how to go
   Through straitest places. Nothing too steep
Or narrow now, once mind and muscle
   Learned to dance their balancings, combined
Against the misdirections of the snow.
   And soon the ground I gained delivered me
Before your smokeless house, and still
   I failed to read that sign. Through cutting air
Two hawks patrolled the reaches of the day,
   Black silhouettes against the sheen
That blinded me. How should I know
   The cold which tempered that blue steel
Claimed you already, for you were old.

## II

Mindful of your death, I hear the leap
   At life in the *resurrexit* of Bruckner's mass:
For, there, your hope towers whole:
   Within a body one cannot see, it climbs
That spaceless space, the ear's
   Chief mystery and mind's, that probes to know
What sense might feel, could it outgo
   Its own destruction, spiralling tireless
Like these sounds. To walk would be enough
   And top that rise behind your house
Where the land lies sheer to Wales,
   And Severn's crescent empties and refills
Flashing its sign inland, its pulse
   Of light that shimmers off the Atlantic:
For too long, age had kept you from that sight
   And now it beats within my eye, its pressure
A reply to the vein's own music
   Here, where with flight-lines interlinking
That sink only to twine and hover the higher,

317

A circling of hawks recalls to us our chains
And snow remaining hardens above your grave.

### III

You wanted a witness that the body
    Time now taught you to distrust
Had once been good. 'My face,' you said—
    And the Shulamite stirred in decembering flesh
As embers fitfully relit—'My face
    Was never beautiful, but my hair
(It reached then to my knees) was beautiful.'
    We met for conversation, not conversion,
For you were that creature Johnson bridled at—
    A woman preacher. With age, your heresies
Had so multiplied that even I
    A pagan, pleaded for poetry forgone:
You thought the telling-over of God's names
    Three-fold banality, for what you sought
Was single, not (and the flame was in your cheek)
    'A nursery rhyme, a jingle for theologians.'
And the incarnation? That, too, required
    All of the rhetoric that I could bring
To its defence. The frozen ground
    Opened to receive you a slot in snow,
Re-froze, and months unborn now wait
    To take you into the earthdark disincarnate.

### IV

A false spring. By noon the frost
    Whitens the shadows only and the stones
Where they lie away from light. The fields
    Give back an odour out of earth
Smoking up through the haysmells where the hay
—I thought it was sunlight in its scattered brightness—
Brings last year's sun to cattle wintering:
    The dark will powder them with white, and day
Discover the steaming herd, as beam
    On beam, and bird by bird, it thaws
Towards another noon. *Et resurrexit:*
    All will resurrect once more,
But whether you will rise again—unless
    To enter the earthflesh and its fullness
Is to rise in the unending metamorphosis
    Through soil and stem . . . This valediction is a requiem.

318

What was the promise to Abraham and his seed?
  That they should feed an everlasting life
In earthdark and in sunlight on the leaf
  Beyond the need of hope or help. But we
Would hunger in hope at the shimmer of a straw,
  Although it burned, a mere memory of fire,
Although the beauty of earth were all there were.

## V

In summer's heat, under a great tree
  I hear the hawks cry down.
The beauty of earth, the memory of your fire
  Tell of a year gone by and more
Bringing the leaves to light: they spread
  Between these words and the birds that hang
Unseen in predatory flight. Again,
  Your high house is in living hands
And what we were saying there is what was said.
  My body measures the ground beneath me
Warm in this beech-foot shade, my verse
  Pacing out the path I shall not follow
To where you spoke once with a wounded
  And wondering contempt against your flock,
Your mind crowded with eagerness and anger.
  The hawks come circling unappeasably. Their clangor
Seems like the energy of loss. It is hunger.
  It pierces and pieces together, a single note,
The territories they come floating over now:
  The escarpment, the foreshore and the sea;
The year that has been, the year to be;
  Leaf on leaf, a century's increment
That has quickened and weathered, withered on the tree
  Down into this brown circle where the shadows thicken.

## The Recompense

                    The night of the comet,
        Sunset gone, and shadow drawing down
      Into itself landscape, horizon, sky,
        We climbed the darkness. Touch
      Was all we had to see by, as we felt
        For a path among the crowding trees:

Somehow, we threaded them, came through
 At last to the vantage we had aimed for:
It was viewless: a sole star,
 The cold space round which seemed
The arena a comet might be found
 Sparkling and speeding through, if only
One waited long enough. We waited.
 No comet came, and no flame thawed
The freezing reaches of our glance: loneliness
 Quelled all we saw—the wide
Empire of that nightworld held
 To the sway of centuries, sidereal law,
And the silent darkness hiding every star
 Save one: had we misheard the date?
A comet, predicted, might be late
 By days perhaps? Chilled, but unwillingly
We took the tree-way down; and ran
 Once feet, freed from obstruction,
Could feel out the smoothest path for us
 From wood to warmth. Now that we faced away
From the spaces we had scanned for light,
 A growing glow rose up to us,
Brought the horizon back once more
 Night had expunged: it travelled contrary
To any comet, this climbing brightness:
 We wound the sight towards us as we went,
The immense circle of the risen moon
 Travelling to meet us: trees
Wrote themselves out on sea and continent,
 A cursive script where every loop and knot
Glimmered in hieroglyph, clear black:
 We—recompense for a comet lost—
Could read ourselves into those lines
 Pulsating on the eye and to the veins,
Thrust and countercharge to our own racing down,
 Lunar flights of the rooted horizon.


## Poem

It falls onto my page like rain
the morning here
and the ink-marks run
to a smoke and stain, a vine-cord, hair:

this script that untangles itself
out of wind, briars, stars unseen,
keeps telling me what I mean
is theirs, not mine:

I try to become all ear
to contain their story:
it goes on arriving from everywhere:
it overflows me

and then:
a bird's veering
into sudden sun
finds me for a pen

a feather on grass,
a blade tempered newly
and oiled to a gloss
dewless among dew:

save for a single
quicksilver drop—
one from a constellation
pearling its tip


## *In April*

I thought that the north
wind was treating the wood
as a thunder-sheet it was
thunder itself had
merged with the roar
of the air in a vast
voice a judgement chord
and the winter that would not go
was blocking spring
through the upper sky piling
ledges of cold onto
ridges of ripening warmth
quaking across the entire
expanse and pushing sun
back into a livid

pre-world light as it
rolled end and beginning
up in a single emphatic
space-travelling verb breath word


## The Order of Saying

'As soon as the blackthorn comes in flower
   The wind blows cold,' she says:
I see those bushes tossed and whitening,
   Drawing the light and currents of the air
Into their mass and depth; can only see
   The order of her saying in that flare
That rises like a beacon for the wind
   To flow into, to twist and wear
Garment and incandescence, flag of spring.


## The Lesson

The larks, this year,
fly so early and so high,
it means, you tell me, summer
will be dry and hot,
and who am I
to gainsay that prophecy?
For twenty years here have not
taught me to read with accuracy
the signs either of earth or sky:
I still keep the eye of a newcomer,
a townsman's eye:
but there is time yet
to better my instruction
in season and in song:
summer on summer

# Hay

The air at evening thickens with a scent
That walls exude and dreams turn lavish on—
Dark incense of a solar sacrament
Where, laid in swathes, the field-silk dulls and dries
To contour out the land's declivities
With parallels of grass, sweet avenues:
Scent hangs perpetual above the changes,
As when the hay is turned and we must lose
This clarity of sweeps and terraces
Until the bales space out the slopes again
Like scattered megaliths. Each year the men
Pile them up close before they build the stack,
Leaving against the sky, as night comes on,
A hedge of hay-bales to confuse the track
Of time, and out of which the smoking dews
Draw odours solid as the huge deception.

# The Conspiracy

My writing hand moves washed in the same light now
   As the beasts in the field beneath this window:
The hot day hangs in the glitter and the shade:
   Those toys of Arden, seeing and half-seeing,
The rocking of the leaves, the slow berceuse,
   The airs advancing to invade the heat
But warming to a world of ease, all
   Breathe together this conspiracy:
Butterflies tongue the nectaries and summer
   Is hiving time against the centuries.

# The Gate

Someone has set up a gate here
   In this unfenced field. Waiting for its fence
It teases the sight. Is it that one feels half-blind,
   The mind demanding an enclosure that the eye
Cannot supply it with? Or is it an X-ray eye
   One has, melting wall to a nothing,

And the grass greening up at one, that returns
   A look with intimations of a place unspaced
And thus not quite there? The mocked mind,
   Busy with surroundings it can neither bound nor unbind,
Cedes to the eye the pleasure of passing
   Where, between the gate's five bars,
Perpetual seawaves play of innumerable grasses.


## At the Edge

The offscape, the in-folds, secreted
   Water-holes in the boles of trees,
Abandoned bits, this door of water
   On the wood's floor (knock with the breath
And enter a world reverted, a catacomb
   Of branching ways where the roots splay):
Edges are centres: once you have found
   Their lines of force, the least of gossamers
Leads and frees you, nets you a universe
   Whose iridescent weave shines true
Because you see it, but whose centre is not you:
   Through the wheel of a web today I saw
The wren, that mere mouse of a bird
   Hurry from its hole and back again
With such an energy of glancing lightness
   It made me measure all the force unspied
That stirred inside that bank, still
   As it seemed, beside the flashing watercourse
That came straight on contrary to my direction and
   Out of the dereliction of an edge of woodland.


## The Near and the Far

It is autumn and there are no flowers in this desert garden. Open to the breeze and to the light, it gauges near against far and resolves them. For the breeze, that pushes to and fro the shadows of the hanging pods of the catalpa tree, is stirring the dust over hundreds of desert miles, lifting it in a veil before the long mass of the Sandía Mountains and picking to pieces the vapour trails of the jets that scar the high and intense blue. As for the light: it reveals sandy distances, ripening the tints, as shadows lengthen, to dusty reds and deep yellows. Here, in the eyes' immediate reaches, it brings out each facet of bark still armouring the stakes that fence the dry yard. Yet they do not fence it in: the endless streaming of light through the cottonwoods, whose leaves are sapless but dazzling, reaches us from an unseen source, a blinding immensity. The sky is full of crossroads of jet-trails, downy tracks gigantically decaying. At foot level, ants are busy in their moonworld of dust and craters.

This desert garden lies at the town's edge, open to the breath of a thousand miles. The engine of a passing truck grinds by with the silence of desert spaces first surrounding then absorbing it. A train passes. Its siren seems to sound out the distances it is entering and, as it were, creating. Waves of wind are rolling across the sky. And from the cottonwoods come the rattle of their leaves, crepitations, lulls, whispers, splashings, like a sea breaking against shore and jetty, where no shore or jetty ever were, on this dried-up bed of a vanished ocean.

Rooted in dust, what do they feed on, these great trees, whose abundance of falling leaves attests the fullness of their summer? In this desert garden there is no succulence. The spiny plants catch at one's ankles, one's shoes are perpetually powdered over. Cottonwood leaves leap across the ground in the wind, side by side with the cicadas that land with a metallic crashing sound among the already shed foliage.

Red ants, dwarfed by their own gangling shadows, carry high their polished abdomens, rushing out on some frantic mission through the warm dust and its maze of cat- and dogpaw prints, shoeshapes, trails where the hose has been dragged across it. The ant nests are composed of a circular wall of dust like a tiny Celtic fortification raised on the desert. Cruzita will not kill the ants because they are part of a divine and unsoundable dispensation. However, she has stood empty jam jars up to their necks in sand, so that the ants can fall into them if that dispensation permits them to. She, the tutelary spirit of this house and garden, has brought into their enclosure the memory of that wisdom which has made life possible across desert and mesa.

She has lit her morning fire. The piñon of which it is built sends out an upland fragrance of pinewoods over the ragged edges of the suburb. The smoke tells the nostrils of the rarer, cooler autumnal air in those fastnesses, recalls to the mind's eye the mesa villages and the sight of trees growing along the mesa top that, seen from afar, look like the stubble of a beard. The light-blue, rising smoke winding above the house, spreading, perfuming the atmosphere, brings to a lingering resolution in its chord of colour, the blue shadows exploring the heights, the dust-haze that the breeze has lifted and a sense of possibility that, investing space, pours into this garden with the light and air.

# Albuquerque

Driving once more
on Central—though what
it is central to
now the town has spread

up to the foothills—
I caught one thing
out of the past that
still was there—

the Kimo Kinema
built in my birth year—
tile, fresco and cement-adobe—
style, tribal art-deco:

Corbusier
could scarcely have applauded
architecture so little tectonic
or so tawdry

and yet a
pupil of his
aware that this
is neither Ronchamps nor Sabbioneta

is actually here
restoring that memory
of a gone year:
I am antique already

# Jemez

When we were children said
Eva they told us
the trees on the skyline there
—we turned to see
the trees on the skyline there
stand staring down—
were the kachinas and we
believed them but today

if you say to children
the trees on the skyline there
—the skyline trees stand
calling up sap out of rock and sand—
are the kachinas they
reply kachinas?[1]
they're nothing but trees

## Cochiti

The cries
of the eagle
dancers at Cochiti
rise to such a
complete complicity
with the way it is
when eagles
speak what they have to say
that the sky
brings down
over thinning snow
unfurling the black
line of wings
slackening then
tautening them back
to take the thrust
of the wind and mount it
to wander away
above the pocked snow-whitenesses
of plain hills mesas
an eagle

## Abiquiu

Rattlesnakes I've had them
in every room of this house
she said: one
lay there suspended
—it might have been in mid-air—

[1] kachinas: tribal spirits

on the down of a piled rug
as if it were swimming:
then one night
I opened the patio
door and the cat
sat there faced
by a snake: neither
moved but the snake kept up
its warning rattle:
day or night
I wouldn't step
right out there
onto the patio
without looking first:
do you know
it's not from that
tight coil
that a rattler strikes:
it's—she twisted her fingers together—
from a tangle
that has no shape
but I tell you
whatever its reputation
a rattlesnake is a gentleman:
before he strikes he
always lets you know


# *Quarai*

Two dogs
wait for the crumbs
from our desert meal:
they are not importunate
but thoughtful in their anticipation:
I recognize their pondering courtesy
in the custodian—they belong to him—
opening his show for us
—artefacts and a plan
of the vanished pueblo—
under a leaking roof
which come spring days
he must he says mend:

La Purissima Concepcion
where the inquisition spied
for witches and blasphemers
cannot account for him:
it died and dwindled
into sky-roofed sandstone here
through pestilence, famine
drought and massacre
unprepared for this
accommodating gentleness
that says: You
hurry on back
whenever you want to

## Under the Bridge

Where the ranch-house disappeared its garden
seeded and the narcissi
began through a slow mutation
to breed smaller and smaller stars
unimpaired in scent: beside these
the horns of the cala lilies
each scroll protruding an insistent
yellow pistil seem from their scale
and succulent whiteness to belong
to an earlier world:
if there were men in it the trellises
that brace these stanchions
would fit the scale
of their husbandry and
if they made music it would
shudder and rebound
like that which travels down
the metal to the base
of this giant instrument
bedded among teazle, fennel, grass
in a returning wilderness
under the bridge

*San Francisco*

# Cronkhite Beach

They look surreal
you said: you meant
the figures along the cliff
above us that the evening light
was thrusting forward in silhouette as if
the sheer stance of curiosity
—they were all stillness facing out to sea—
had magnified them: wave
after wave was entering
from the horizon: moving mountains
which as they sailed-in threw
the surf backwards from their peaks
each like a separate volcano:
and the diminishing force unspent
you could measure by the pitch
of the off-shore buoy
belling the shallows as the sea
tugged past it to become
white on the darkening beach
a frayed rope of foam: and there
were the peaceful Brobdignagians still
stationed out massively along that hill:
tall as the objects of their contemplation
they looked surreal: so real

# Poolville, N.Y.

*Brekekekex?*
The frogs of upstate speak
with a mellifluousness as ungreek
as their names—'spring peepers':
neither hoarse nor flatulent
like the ones elsewhere, this
breed were never peasantry
like those in Ovid's metamorphosis,
but nature's aristocracy—
'We are all princes here':
and thus will never ask
for a log for king
and end up with a stork:

they must sing four night and then
they've safely brought the springtime in
past tardy drifts and up the trees
to a music that outdates
Ovid and Aristophanes.

# Parsnips

### for Ted Chamberlin

A mixed crop. I dig a clump:
Crotches seamed with soil,
Soil clinging to every hair,
To excrescences and mandrake mandibles.
Poor bare forked earth-stained animals,
One comes up whole and white,
A vegetable Adam. I take the lot
And wash them at the stream.
Rubbing, rinsing, I let fall
Inevitably this image of perfection,
Then rush for a garden rake
To fish it back again and run
Trying to out-race the current's
Rain-fed effervescence:
Fit image of the poet, he
In the waterproof, with the iron comb who goes
Hunting a prey that's halfway to the sea.

# Programme Note

Reading this, you are waiting for the curtain
    To go up on a glade, vistaed valley
Or colonnade of lath. Yet you are not here
    To view a painting—the painted thing
Like the written word, is there for the hearing—
    To which end the tympanist stretches his ear
To interrogate a drumskin, hangs over
    Undistracted by bell note or forest murmur
In horn and harp. Cellist pursues
    An intent colloquy with his instrument,
Urging nerve and string up to that perfection
    He may falter at. For, the aria done,

It is he alone who must comment on
    The meaning of it, and bars he is testing now
Climb then on a faultless bow
    Out of the darkened pit as the hero pauses
To resume in song. He, too, unseen
    Sweating into his paint, runs through
(In mind, that is) the perils of a part
    That from start to finish (and this is true
Of every bubble and iota of these tuning notes)
    Raises its fragment to build a single arc
Of sound. Yet suppose that you are here
    Tonight to share in the good conscience
Of all masquerade, that this wood or square
    Waits to be filled with cadences in which
Taking leave of the humid north,
    The steam of Niebelheim, you find yourself
With time and light enough to feel
    The filigree of things, and dare to be
Superficial out of profundity: suppose
    This composer of yours had for a beginning
The merest ravelled thread of a plot—
    The sort of thing a poet would wince at
Or a bad poet write—, it flows
    Out from his musician's mind, not
As the Gesammtkunstwerk (let that dragon sleep),
    The streambed's deep self-inspection,
But the purest water where reflection
    Pooling for a moment, is drawn along
Over drops and through recesses, to emerge
    Strong though contained, a river of song:
You feel that you could leap it from side to side:
    Its dazzle and deftness so take hold,
They convince the mind that it might be
    Equally agile, equally free:
Are you the swift that dips here, or the course
    Of sheer, unimpeded water, the counterforce
Of rock and stone? But images lie—
    Not the Ding-an-sich, but the light to see it by:
And no river could convey the artifice
    And no landscape either, the pulse of this:
A closer thing, it is as if thought might sing
    To the bloodbeat, set it racing;
As if . . . and yet a man shaped this
    Who read the fragile story from the start

As that which his art would make of it—
   So that, in the mind, the body dances
To this flowing fiction—soprano, tenor
   And basso buffo—believing all,
Limpid, unpsychological: and finding true
   A wholly imaginary passion—passion spaced until
Meted and metred-out, its urgency
   Does not merely billow up to fill
The gallery with sound. But I have said
   Enough and the musicians mouthed and bowed
Their accordant A; the light glows out
   On the gildings, and here is the man in black
And white who holds this world of yellow and green and red
   Together, and his first chord cuts the last whisper back.

## On a Pig's Head

Once it had gorged itself
to a pitch of succulence, they slew it:
it was the stare in the eyes
the butcher hated, and so removed
with a quick knife,
transforming the thing
to a still life, hacked
and halved, cross-cutting it
into angles with ears.
It bled no more,
though the black pearls
still lurked on its rawness.
The ears were streaked with wax,
the teeth stained near the roots
like an inveterate smoker's.
It was the nose looked freshest—
a rubbery, soft pink.
With a spill of paper, I cleaned
the orifice of each ear,
and played water into the nostrils.
The brain was a mere thimble of brain,
and the tongue, smaller than a sheep's
sliced neatly. The severed ears
seemed delicate on their plate
with their maze of veins.

When we submerged it in brine
to change it to brawn and galantine,
it wouldn't fit the bowls:
evidently, it had been conceived
for a more capacious age.
Divided, it remained massive
leaving no room for reflection
save that peppercorns, cloves
of garlic, bay-leaves and wine
would be necessary for its transformation.
When set to boil, it required
a rock, a great
red one
from Macuilxochitl
to keep it down.

## Ritornello

Wrong has a twisty look like wrung misprinted
Consider! and you con the stars for meaning
Sublime comes climbing from beneath the threshold
Experience? you win it out of peril
The pirate's cognate. Where did the words arise?
Human they sublimed out of the humus
Surprised by stars into consideration
You are wrung right and put into the peril
Of feelings not yet charted lost for words
Abstraction means something pulled away from
Humus means earth place purchase and return

## San Fruttuoso:
### the divers

Seasalt has rusted the ironwork trellis
at the one café. Today
the bathers are all sun-bathers
and their bodies, side by side,
hide the minute beach:
the sea is rough and the sun's
rays pierce merely fitfully

an ill-lit sky. Unvisited,
the sellers of lace and postcards
have nothing to do, and the Dorias
in their cool tombs under the cloisters
sleep out history unfleshed.
*Oggi pesce spada*
says the café sign, but we
shall eat no swordfish today:
we leave by the ferry
from which the divers are arriving.
We wait under an orange tree
that produces flowers but no oranges.
They litter the rocks with their gear
and begin to assume
alternative bodies, slipping
into black rubbery skins with *Caution*
written across them.
They are of both sexes. They strap on
waist weights, frog feet,
cylinders of oxygen,
they lean their heaviness which water will lighten
back against rock, resting there
like burdened seals.
They test their cylinders
and the oxygen hisses at them.
They carry knives
and are well equipped to encounter
whatever it is draws them downwards
in their sleek black flesh.
The postcards show Christ—
*Cristo del mare*—
sunk and standing on his pedestal
with two divers circling
as airy as under-water birds
in baroque, ecstatic devotion
round the bad statue.
Will they find calm down there
we wonder, stepping heavily
over the ship-side gap,
feeling already the unbalancing
pull of the water under us.
We pass the granular rocks
faulted with long scars.
The sea is bristling up to them.

The straightness of the horizon
as we heave towards it
only disguises the intervening
sea-roll and sea-chop, the clutching glitter.
I rather like
the buck of the boat. What I dislike
with the sea tilting at us
is the thought of losing one's brains
as one slides sideways
to be flung at the bulwarks
as if weightless, the 'as if'
dissolving on impact
into bone and blood.
The maternal hand tightens
on the push-chair
that motion is dragging at:
her strapped-in child is asleep.
Perhaps those invisible divers—
luckier than we are—
all weight gone
levitate now
around the statue,
their corps de ballet
like Correggio's sky-
swimming angels, a swarm
of batrachian legs:
they are buoyed up by adoration,
the water merely an accidental aid
to such staggeringly
slow-motion pirouettes
forgetful of body, of gravity.
The sea-lurch snatches
and spins the wheels of his chair
and the child travels the sudden gradient
caught at by other hands,
reversed in mid-flight
and returned across the up-
hill deck to his mother:
a visitor,
she has the placid
and faintly bovine look
of a Northern madonna
and is scarcely surprised; he, too,
stays perfectly collected

aware now of what it was he had forgotten
while sleeping—the stuff
he was chewing from a packet,
which he continues to do.
He has come back to his body once more.
How well he inhabits his flesh:
lordly in unconcern,
he is as well accoutred as those divers.
He rides out the storm chewing and watching,
trustfully unaware
we could well go down
—though we do not, for already
the town is hanging above
us and the calm quay water.
From the roofs up there
perhaps one could see the divers
emerging, immersing,
whatever it is they are at
as we glide forward
up to the solid, deck to dock,
with salted lips.
That same sea
which wrecked Shelley
goes on rocking behind
and within us, hiding
its Christ, its swordfish,
as the coast reveals
a man-made welcome to us
of wall, street, room,
body's own measure and harbour,
shadow of lintel, portal
asking it in.


## *Above Carrara*

### *for Paolo and Francesco*

Climbing to Colonnata past ravines
   Squared by the quarryman, geometric gulfs
Stepping the steep, the wire and gear
   Men use to pare a mountain: climbing
With the eye the absences where green should be,
   The annihilating scree, the dirty snow

Of marble, at last we gained a level
  In the barren flat of a piazza, leaned
And drank from the fountain there a jet
  As cold as tunneled rock. The place—
Plane above plane and block on block—
  Invited us to climb once more
And, cooled now, so we did
  Deep between church- and house-wall,
Up by a shadowed stairway to emerge
  Where the village ended. As we looked back then
The whole place seemed a quarry for living in,
  And between the acts of quarrying and building
To set a frontier, a nominal petty thing,
  While, far below, water that cooled our thirst
Dyed to a meal now, a sawdust flow,
  Poured down to slake those blades
Slicing inching the luminous mass away
  Above Carrara . . .


# *Fireflies*

The signal light of the firefly in the rose:
Silent explosions, low suffusions, fire
Of the flesh-tones where the phosphorous touches
On petal and on fold: that close world lies
Pulsing within its halo, glows or goes:
But the air above teems with the circulation
Of tiny stars on darkness, cosmos grows
Out of their circlings that never quite declare
The shapes they seem to pin-point, swarming there
Like stitches of light that fleck and thread a sea,
Yet unlike, too, in that the dark is spaces,
Its surfaces all surfaces seen through,
Discovered depths, filled by a flowering,
And though the rose lie lost now to the eye,
You could suppose the whole of darkness a forming rose.

## Thunder in Tuscany

Down the façade lean statues listening:
Ship of the lightning-gust, ship of the night,
The long nave draws them into dark, they glisten
White in the rainflash, to shudder-out blackbright:
The threads of lightning net and resinew form
In sudden fragments—line of a mouth, a hem—
Taut with the intent a body shapes through them
Standing on sheerness outlistening the storm.

## Giovanni Diodati

*from the Italian of Attilio Bertolucci*

My astonishment almost felicity
when I discovered Giovanni Diodati—
whose protestant Bible which I was reading
somehow entered my household—Catholic

if only tepidly with tenacious roots—
was the friend of that John Milton
whom today—late—I count among those poets
I care for most. The shimmer

of his lines—when he depicts Eve naked
garnishing a cloth
with reddening fruits in the autumn
of Paradise its noonday corruscating

at the guest's approach—Raphael
the Archangel—for a meal for three—
isn't it just the same as in the prose
of the exile from Lucca beside Lake Leman

where the Bride of the Canticle appears
suggesting to the intent adolescent—
fiery twilight coming slantwise in
to the resonant granary of wheat
hiding-place in air vertigo

of a plain black with swallows—the saliva of kisses?

# On a May Night

*after the prose of Leopardi's journal*

Gloom in my mind: I leaned
at a window that showed the square:
two youths on the grass-grown
steps before the abandoned church
fooling and falling around
sat there beneath the lamp: appears
the first firefly of that year:
and one of them's up already
to set on it: I ask
within myself mercy for the poor thing
urging it *Go go* but he
battered and beat it low then turned
back to his friend: meantime
the coachman's daughter
comes up to a window
to wash a platter
and turning tells those within
*Tonight it will rain*
*no matter what:*
*it's as black as a hat out there*
and then the light at that
window vanishes: the firefly
in the interval has come round:
I wanted to—but the youth
found it was moving turned
swore and another
blow laid out the creature
and with his foot he made
a shining streak of it
across the dust until
he'd rubbed it out: arrived
a third youth from an alley-way
fronting the church
who was kicking the stones and
muttering: the killer laughingly
leaps at him bringing him down
then lifts him bodily:
as the game goes on
the din dies but the loud
laughs come volleying through:

I heard the soft voice
of a woman I neither knew nor saw:
*Let's go Natalino: it's late:*
*For godsake* he replies
*it isn't daybreak yet:* I heard
a child that must surely be
hers and carried by her
babblingly rehearse
in a milky voice
inarticulate laughing sounds
just now and then out of its own
quite separate universe: the fun
flares up again: *Is there any*
*wine to spare at Girolamo's?*
they ask of someone passing:
wine there was none:
the woman began laughing softly
trying out
proverbs that might fit
the situation: and yet that wine
was not for her and that
money would be
coin purloined from the family
by her husband:
and every so often she
repeated with a laughing patience
her hint *Let's go*
in vain: at last a cry
*Oh look* comes from them
*it's raining:* it was a light spring rain:
and all withdrew bound homewards:
you could hear the sound
of doors of bolts
and this scene
which pleased drawing me from myself
appeased me.

# Instead of an Essay

### for Donald Davie

Teacher and friend, what you restored to me
Was love of learning; and without that gift
A cynic's bargain could have shaped my life
To end where it began, in detestation
Of the place and man that had mistaught me.
You were the first to hear my poetry,
Written above a bay in Italy:
Lawrence and Shelley found a refuge once
On that same coast—exiles who had in common
Love for an island slow to learn of it
Or to return that love. And so had we
And do—you from the far shore of the sea
And I beside a stream in Gloucestershire
That feeds it. Meeting maybe once a year
We take the talk up where we left it last,
Forgetful of which fashions, tide on tide—
The buddha, shamanism, suicide—
Have come and passed.
Brother in a mystery you trace
To God, I to an awareness of delight
I cannot name, I send these lines to you
In token of the prose I did not write.

# Barque Nornen

Barque Nornen broken by the storms
vanishes in shifting sand:
tides reshape the terrain and
unsilt the ship's clear hollow form:

Berrow church-tower looks out on
the ruin of that other nave
its sides like an inverted wave
and rib on rib as hard as stone.

# The Littleton Whale

*in memory of Charles Olson*

What you wrote to know
was whether
the old ship canal
still paralleled the river
south
of Gloucester (England) . . .

What I never told
in my reply
was of the morning
on that same stretch
(it was a cold
January day in '85)
when Isobel Durnell
saw the whale . . .

She was up at dawn
to get her man off on time
to the brickyard and
humping up over the banks
beyond Bunny Row
a slate-grey hill showed
that the night before
had not been there . . .

They both ran outside
and down to the shore:
the wind was blowing
as it always blows
so hard that the tide
comes creeping up under it
often unheard . . .

The great grey-blue thing
had an eye
that watched wearily
their miniature motions as they
debated its fate
for the tide
was already feeling beneath it
floating it away . . .

343

It was Moses White
master mariner
owner of the sloop *Matilda*
who said the thing to do
was to get chains and a traction engine
—they got two from Olveston—
and drag it ashore:
the thing was a gift:
before long it would be
drifting off to another part of the coast
and lost to them
if they didn't move now . . .

And so the whale—
flukes, flesh, tail
trembling no longer
with a failing life—
was chained and hauled
installed above the tideline . . .

And the crowds came
to where it lay
upside down
displaying a
belly evenly-wrinkled
its eye lost to view
mouth skewed and opening into
an interior of tongue and giant sieves
that had once
filtered that diet of shrimp
its deep-sea sonar
had hunted out for it
by listening to submarine echoes
too slight
for electronic selection . . .

And Hector Knapp
wrote in his diary:
Thear was a Whal
cum ashore at Littleton Pill
and bid thear a fortnight
He was sixty eaight feet long

His mouth was twelve feet
The Queen claim it at last
and sould it for forty pound
Thear supposed to be
forty thousen pepeal to se it
from all parts of the cuntry ...

The Methodist preacher
said that George Sindry
who was a very religious man
told himself when that whale came in
he'd heard so many arguments
about the tale of Jonah not being true
that he went to Littleton to
'satisfy people'. He was a tall man
a six footer
'but I got into that whale's mouth' he said
'and I stood in it
upright ...'

The carcass
had overstayed its welcome
so they sent up a sizeable boat
to tow it to Bristol
and put it on show there
before they cut the thing down stinking
to be sold
and spread for manure ...

You can still see the sign
to Whale Wharf as they renamed it
and Wintle's Brickworks became
the Whale Brick
Tile and Pottery Works ...

Walking daily onto
the now-gone premises
through the 'pasture land
with valuable deposits of clay thereunder'
when the machine- and drying sheds

the five kilns, the stores and stables
stood permanent in that place
of their disappearance
Enoch Durnell still
relished his part in all that history begun
when Bella shook
and woke him with a tale that the tide
had washed up a whole house
with blue slates on it into Littleton Pill
and that house was a whale . . .

# The Flood

It was the night of the flood first took away
   My trust in stone. Perfectly reconciled it lay
Together with water—and does so still—
   In the hill-top conduits that feed into
Cisterns of stone, cisterns echoing
   With a married murmur, as either finds
Its own true note in such a unison.
   It rained for thirty days. Down chimneys
And through doors, the house filled up
   With the roar of waters. The trees were bare,
With nothing to keep in the threat
   And music of that climbing, chiming din
Now rivers ran where the streams once were.
   Daily, we heard the distance lessening
Between house and water-course. But floods
   Occur only along the further plains and we
Had weathered the like of this before
   —The like, but not the equal, as we saw,
Watching it lap the enclosure wall,
   Then topping it, begin to pile across
And drop with a splash like clapping hands
   And spread. It took in the garden
Bed by bed, finding a level to its liking.
   The house-wall, fronting it, was blind
And therefore safe: it was the doors
   On the other side unnerved my mind
—They and the deepening night. I dragged
   Sacks, full of a mush of soil
Dug in the rain, and bagged each threshold.

Spade in hand, why should I not make
Channels to guide the water back
    Into the river, before my barricade
Proved how weak it was? So I began
    Feeling my way into the moonless rain,
Hacking a direction. It was then as though
    A series of sluices had been freed to overflow
All the land beneath them: it was the dark I dug
    Not soil. The sludge melted away from one
And would not take the form of a trench.
    This work led nowhere, with no bed
To the flood, no end to its sources and resources
    To grow and to go wherever it would
Taking one with it. It was the sound
    Struck more terror than the groundlessness I trod,
The filth fleeing my spade—though that, too,
    Carried its image inward of the dissolution
Such sound orchestrates—a day
    Without reprieve, a swealing away
Past shape and self. I went inside.
    Our ark of stone seemed warm within
And welcoming, yet echoed like a cave
    To the risen river whose tide already
Pressed close against the further side
    Of the unwindowed wall. There was work to do
Here better than digging mud—snatching
    And carrying such objects as the flood
Might seep into, putting a stair
    Between the world of books and water.
The mind, once it has learned to fear
    Each midnight eventuality,
Can scarcely seize on what is already there:
    It was the feet first knew
The element weariness had wandered through
    Eyeless and unreasoning. Awakened eyes
Told that the soil-sacked door
    Still held, but saw then, without looking,
Water had tried stone and found it wanting:
    Wall fountained a hundred jets:
Floor lay awash, an invitation
    To water to follow it deriding door
On door until it occupied the entire house.
    We bailed through an open window, brushing
And bucketing with a mindless fervour

347

As though four hands could somehow find
Strength to keep pace, then oversway
    The easy redundance of a mill-race. I say
That night diminished my trust in stone—
    As porous as a sponge, where once I'd seen
The image of a constancy, a ground for the play
    And fluency of light. That night diminished
Yet did not quite betray my trust.
    For the walls held. As we tried to sleep,
And sometimes did, we knew that the flood
    Rivered ten feet beneath us. And so we hung
Between a dream of fear and the very thing.
    Water-lights coursed the brain and sound
Turned it to the tympanum of an ear. When I rose
    The rain had ceased. Full morning
Floated and raced with water through the house,
    Dancing in whorls on every ceiling
As I advanced. Sheer foolishness
    It seemed to pause and praise the shimmer
And yet I did and called you down
    To share this vertigo of sunbeams everywhere,
As if no surface were safe from swaying
    And the very stone were as malleable as clay.
Primeval light undated the day
    Back into origin, washed past stain
And staleness, to a beginning glimmer
    That stilled one's beating ear to sound
Until the flood-water seemed to stream
    With no more burden than the gleam itself.
Light stilled the mind, then showed it what to do
    Where the work of an hour or two could
Hack a bank-side down, let through
    The stream and thus stem half the force
That carried its weight and water out of course.
    Strength spent, we returned. By night
The house was safe once more, but cold within.
    The voice of waters burrowed one's dream
Of ending in a wreck of walls:
    We were still here, with too much to begin
That work might make half-good.
    We waited upon the weather's mercies
And the December stars frosted above the flood.

348

# Severnside

We looked for the tide, for the full river
  Riding up the expanse to the further cliff:
But its bed lay bare—sand
  That a brisk wind planed towards us.
Perpetual shore it seemed, stretch
  And invitation to all we could see and more:
Hard to think of it as the thoroughfare for shoals:
  At the edge, a cracked mosaic of mud,
Even shards of it dried in the sunny wind—
  A wind whose tidal sound mocked tidelessness,
Mocked, too, the grounded barges grass now occupied
  Dense on the silt-filled holds. Sad,
But a glance told you that land had won,
  That we would see no swell today
Impelled off the Atlantic, shelving
  And channelling riverwards in the hour we had.
And so we turned, and the wind possessed our ears,
  Mocked on, and our talk turned, too,
Mind running on future things,
  Null to all save the blind pull of muscle
In a relegated present. When we paused
  The sands were covered and the channels full:
We had attended the wind too long, robbed
  Of distinction between the thing it was
And what it imitated. But the rise we stood on,
  Reawakening our eyes, gave back suddenly
More than the good that we had forfeited:
  Ahead—below—we could sight now
The present, as it were, spread to futurity
  And up the river's bend and bed
The waters travelling, a prow of light
  Pushing the foam before them in its onrush
Over the waiting sand. And we who seemed
  To be surfing forward on that white
Knew that we only dreamed of standing still
  Here where a tide whose coming we had missed
Rode massed before us in the filled divide.

# In the Estuary

This is the way it goes, the tide:
   A stain through the water, a first sign
That the light is getting down to layers
   Under the flowing surface: then
Colour brought up out of the depths
   To reveal suddenly a ledge of sand
Turning into a glassy island that reflects
   The further shore. The swimming birds
Are left standing, and walk to and fro
   Across their mirrored landscape, each
Accompanying its own white reflection.
   The channel shallowing, two rocks
(To begin with) and then a chain
   Of rock on rock, space out an archipelago
Of islets before the continental mass
   Which was the sand. You could not map
This making and unmaking. Every gap
   Is losing water. Every rise
Tussocked with grass that greens and fattens
   In the tidal flow, shows now
As an inland island above mudflats
   Through which the veins of channels hurry-off
What's left of the river from its bed.
   Reading the weather from such skies—
Cloud promise and cloud countermand—
   As cover this searun neither sea nor land,
You end in contraries like the bight itself,
   Where an unseen moon is pulling the place from focus
And the lunar ripple runs woven with the sunlight.

# The Epilogue

It was a dream delivered the epilogue:
   I saw the world end: I saw
Myself and you, tenacious and exposed,
   Smallest insects on the largest leaf:
A high trail coasted a ravine
   Eyes could not penetrate because a wood
Hung down its slope: a fugue of water
   Startled the ear and air with distances

Around and under us, as if a flood
    Came pouring in from every quarter:
Our trail and height failed suddenly,
    Fell sheer away into a visibility
More terrible than what the trees might hide:
    Fed by a fall, wide, rising
Was it a sea? claimed all the plain
    And climbed towards us, smooth
And ungainsayable. We turned and knew now
    That no law steadied a sliding world,
For what we saw was an advancing wave
    Cresting along the height. An elate
Despair held us together silent there
    Waiting for that wall to fall and bury
Us and the love that taught us to forget
    To fear it. I woke then to this room
Where first I heard the sounds that dogged that dream,
    Caught back from epilogue to epilogue.

Throughout thirty years Charles Tomlinson's poetry often seems to be moving between two poles — England and America, country and town, home and abroad, nature and history. There is also a religious element in his work as he looks for openings through place into mystery. Place has spoken to Tomlinson of fundamental things — time, death, what we have in common with the animals, what Eden is like, what a centre is. This Eden is always poised over against a world of political and historical change, and if Tomlinson is a landscape poet, he is also the poet of Marat's and Trotsky's assassinations and of Lenin's take-over. Fundamentally — and before public concern expressed itself on the matter — this has long been an ecological poetry in the sense that the act of attention it has always involved grows out of a reverence for the natural world and a distrust of the unfeeling human will that would inflict violence upon it. This will is also seen at work and criticized by the poet in the political realm. Not that there are any politically partisan poems here. Our right relation to the world is suggested by Tomlinson in his creation of a poetic freshness, even a certain sunniness of atmosphere which is no enemy to wit, humour or emotion. As Donald Davie has written of his most recent collection, *Notes from New York*: 'He insists, and he has a right to insist, that he is as authentic a voice of modern Britain as Philip Larkin is, . . . If *Notes from New York* gives us the poet in relaxed mood, it is a great poet who thus relaxes. . . . Only in the great poets is content so intimately married to form.'

'Charles Tomlinson is the first poet to have learned a way of being distinctly English by mastering an idiom markedly international. Consequently he can write English, in England, as though it were a foreign tongue of amazing resources, at his thorough if somewhat wary command. Flaubert had learned to write French in a similar spirit.'                    Hugh Kenner.

'Very few poets alive write so consistently well, and very few have been so experimental in rhythms inside the main stream of the English language.' Peter Levi.